CONSERVATIVE CHIC

CONSERVATIVE CHIC

The 5-Step Program for Dressing with Style

BY AMELIA FATT

Illustrations by Song Finger

Times
BOOKS

Published by TIMES BOOKS, a division of
The New York Times Book Co., Inc.
Three Park Avenue, New York, N.Y. 10016

Published simultaneously in Canada by
Fitzhenry & Whiteside, Ltd., Toronto

Library of Congress Cataloging in Publication Data

Fatt, Amelia.
  Conservative chic.

  1. Clothing and dress. 2. Fashion. I. Finger, Song.
II. Title.
TT507.F363   1983   646'.34   82-40368
ISBN 0-8129-1041-9
ISBN 0-8129-6328-8 (pbk.)

Manufactured in the United States of America
83 84 85 86 87 5 4 3 2 1

Design by Pat Stuppi

To my mother, whose love of beautiful clothes and enthusiasm for a ladylike look were the earliest influences on the ideas in this book

ACKNOWLEDGMENTS

My thanks to Catherine Heiser for the help she gave me with the cut and fabric sections, and to Amy Gross and my husband, Larry Plapler, for their opinions and encouragement.

CONTENTS

CHAPTER SEVEN

CHAPTER EIGHT

CHAPTER NINE

Grooming and Clothing Care   167

CHAPTER TEN

Conservative Chic on a Shoestring   169

CONSERVATIVE
CHIC

I am a personal fashion consultant. For eight years, I have dressed younger women and older women, working women and housewives and ladies of leisure, wealthy women and women on very limited incomes, blondes and redheads and brunettes, pretty women and plain women, women who love clothes and women who hate them.

At the very least, I influence what my client reaches into the closet for each morning. At my most influential, I redesign and redefine her entire appearance. This is heady stuff—and a great responsibility. If a woman entrusts me with something as personal as her appearance, I want to help her look her very best.

People often say to me, "But I thought all women loved to shop!" This stereotype is responsible for many women's feeling inadequate or unfeminine. It's as ridiculous to assume all women are avid and competent shoppers as it is to assume all men are reluctant and incompetent ones.

In fact, lots of women loathe shopping—because they simply are not interested in it, or because they find it fatiguing, or because they find it increasingly difficult to locate the kind of clothes they might live happily ever after in. Yet many women express a great reluctance to delegate this task to a professional. They are afraid of losing their individuality—afraid they'll end up looking like everyone else.

I understand that concern, and I can tell you a couple of things about my work that might reassure you. In the first place, I view what I do as a collaboration between me and my client. She will be wearing the clothes, so she must be comfortable in them—they must express something about *her,* even if that something is not what she has emphasized in the past. Secondly, I went into this work because I feel there are individual solutions to individual problems, and an individual solution is what I look for. I would get bored if I chose the same thing for everyone (even if the same thing would work, which it wouldn't). As a matter of fact, many of my clients find—and I think you would, too—that they actually look more individual *after* we have worked together.

In case you may be wondering, I don't believe appearance is everything. If I send you to an important job interview looking businesslike and successful, yet you aren't qualified for the job, I don't believe you will land it just on the strength of your appearance. But, if you *are* qualified, I can help prevent you from losing it on the weakness of your appearance. For it is a fact of life that people who look attractive do get a more positive initial response. And knowing you look your best can add to your feeling of self-confidence in situations where you sense you are under scrutiny.

Many of my customers have told me that the greatest dividend they received from my help was that feeling of relaxation about their appearance—that they could forget about it and turn their attention to their work, interests, or whatever. And, once in a while, a client will tell me that the changes she made in her appearance gave her the courage to make other changes as well, and that those changes made her life happier and fuller. This doesn't always happen, of course, but when it does it is very gratifying.

I often find that curiosity about what I do is coupled with curiosity about what makes clients seek my help. As I'll explain to you in the next chapter, there are as many reasons a woman might call on me as there are women who do. One of the most interesting things about my work is the variety of women I deal with.

Yet, in one respect, that last statement is not entirely accurate. Over the years, I have discovered that my many and various clients share one trait: Every one of them describes the way she wishes to look as "conservative."

Not all of them use the word "conservative." Some say "classic," some say "untrendy," some say "elegant." But they all mean the same thing: conservative. At first I was amused . . . then amazed.

Did such an overwhelming consensus of opinion indicate some peculiarity of my clientele—a political leaning, perhaps? None that I could discover.

What I did discover is that most women want to look conservative most of the time—regardless of what's in fashion.

In the beginning I worried a lot about this. I worried that when my clients said conservative they meant it in the negative sense: safe, dull, unimaginative, invisible. I couldn't imagine why they would hire me for such a negative purpose; I worried that my work would not be fun.

I was wrong. Dull outfits were rejected when I included them to hedge my bets. "Sensible" but unbecoming styles and "basic" colors that do nothing for you don't belong in anyone's wardrobe.

Slowly, customer by customer, I developed a sense of what my clients meant by conservative, and it wasn't dull, unimaginative, or invisible. It was actually a style that I was trying to steer them toward anyway, although at that time *I* might not have called it conservative. Such a style had all the conservative virtues—it didn't date easily, raised no eyebrows socially or in the business world, was age-appropriate, was elegant, was dignified, and was subtly enhancing rather than overwhelming to the woman who wore it. But it was also chic. Without ever looking trendy, my clients were always stylish. Other women, and men, commented on how beautifully they dressed.

When I realized that all my customers wanted to look conservative, I began to think about writing this book. Before that, I worried about making the generalizations that would be necessary in order to write a how-to-dress book. As I said, I went into this kind of work because I believe in individual solutions to individual problems. I hated all those articles in fashion magazines that encourage you to type yourself and thereby find the solution to your problem. I never fit into the categories they offered; neither did my clients.

I still believe in individual solutions, but my awareness of my clients' preference for a conservative look has led me to realize that I do have a particular technique for achieving such a look in an individualized and stylish way. This book is an explanation of my technique, which can be broken down into five steps, and of the kind of work I do for my individual clients. But, even more, it is a description of a way of thinking about clothes that yielded the technique in the first place. It is this way of thinking about clothes that is the most valuable skill I can impart to you, for with it you can solve just about any clothing problem, including some I may not have mentioned in this book.

Do you picture conservative dressing as dowdy, dreary—a series of "uniforms" that allow you no self-expression?

You have the wrong conservative look.

Let me introduce you to *Conservative Chic*.

CHAPTER ONE

What Is Conservative Chic?

One of the questions I used to ask a new client was whether there was someone in the public eye, such as a movie star or a very successful businesswoman, whose style or look she particularly liked. I could see the wheels turning as each woman gave the question her careful consideration, but responses were scant and unrevealing. And when a client did come up with someone, I always felt she arrived at her choice more to give me what she thought I wanted than to express something about herself.

I had hoped the answer to this question would give me a picture of how my client aspired to look, but it never did. Chalking it up as just another example of something that should work but doesn't, I stopped asking it. Eventually, the answer to this question dawned on me as well as the reason why it yielded so little information.

The woman my client wants to look like is never a movie star or public figure—she is always someone she knows, someone around her own age whom she socializes or works with. Attractive, but not necessarily beautiful, this enviable creature is always beautifully dressed and, without apparent effort, looks right for the time, the place, the group. Her clothes are never the last shriek of fashion, but her look is definitely chic; she may or may not have money, but she does have a lot of style.

You probably know and admire such a woman yourself. Movie stars and fashion models may excite and inspire us, but when we choose someone to emulate, she is usually closer to home. Who she is and how she looks seem within our reach—or just beyond it. She is an idealized version of ourselves.

It was often at lunch, after we had spent the morning shopping together, that a client would bring up this admired friend or acquaintance. And because the same adjectives kept popping up whenever her name did, I began to get a picture of this paragon: "Feminine without being frilly . . . well-groomed and correct wherever she goes . . . never seems stiff or uncomfortable in her clothing . . . youthful but not juvenile . . . clothes that are put together well." She has her own style and her own look—but that style is always described as conservative.

That word again! What did it mean to all these women who had sought me out for so many different reasons? Women who had no time to shop, or no sense of what looked good on them; women I dressed year after year, or who hired me once as a special treat; women who were working, returning to work, or had never worked; women who were newly married or newly single. In one week, I might hear it from an investment banker, a Westchester housewife, and an actress.

Conservative

My clients redefined this word for me by sharing with me their feelings about how they wanted to look.

In the first place, no woman wants to look ridiculous. No one wants to be what *Women's Wear Daily* snidely refers to as a "fashion victim," someone who buys and wears the latest look no matter how poorly it suits her appearance.

This is a genuine concern. Most of us don't aspire to be on the cutting edge of fashion. While we admire the fashion model draped in twenty scarves, we don't really wish to be her. She probably doesn't wear twenty scarves in real life, either. Fashion magazines use exaggeration to make a point—they show twenty scarves to lead you to the concept of wearing two. My clients were afraid they couldn't carry many of the "fashionable" looks they saw in magazines and in the stores—and they were right.

So the first thing conservative means is not ridiculous. Next, my clients want to look and be comfortable physically as well as emotionally in what they wear. I quickly found that no woman looked good, or felt she looked good, in clothes that didn't fit properly, move easily, or bear some resemblance to her own idea of herself, her body shape, and her sense of what she could carry off.

The second thing conservative means is age-appropriate. No client is interested in looking much younger or older than she really is. If she is older, she wants to look a youthful whatever-her-age; if she is very young, she might wish to look a bit more grown-up or authoritative, but not as if she were wearing her mother's clothes.

The third thing conservative means is dressing in accordance with your lifestyle: looking in tune with your kind of work, your job status, and the people with whom you socialize. If you are a lawyer, you should look like one. If you work in advertising, you may have more leeway in how you dress but you still have to look like a businesswoman. If you are a woman with heavy social responsibilities, you should dress in tune with the people you socialize with.

The fourth thing conservative means is looking right for the part of the country you live in. Corporate wives from various parts of the country frequently arrive in New York worried about having an "out-of-town" look. One client, fresh from a small Southern city, showed me a summer wardrobe of splashy flower prints in hot pastels (bright pink, bright blue, bright green, etc.), several pairs of white shoes, and a handbag with a frog embroidered on it. I had to tell her that sophisticated New Yorkers rarely if ever wear white shoes in summer, generally wear hot pastels in smaller doses, and have a different concept of a handbag. She ended up with bone shoes, smaller prints in more subtle colors, and a handbag without an animal on it—and her husband received a number of compliments on how well his wife dressed (even when they went home to visit).

I don't have to wonder why my clients prefer to look conservative. They have a number of excellent reasons:

1. *They want to look businesslike for their work.* Women *should* look conservative in most working situations. And they can achieve a businesslike appearance through a number of routes, although dressing as much like a man as possible is not one of them. Young women in entry-level positions and women re-entering the job market are most concerned about dressing effectively. Women who have "arrived," who already hold executive or professional positions, are more relaxed. But all of them feel they have to look conservative.

Not all of them are happy about this, of course. One beautiful, sexy new lawyer practically wept when she told me how unhappy she was about spending money on appropriately conservative clothes for work, because she was certain she would feel ugly in them. Finding the right clothes for her was a real challenge—that was the season when just about everything came slit up to the thigh, and I did not think it would further her career to call attention to her spectacular legs. An exhaustive search finally yielded a wardrobe of conservatively cut clothes in subtle colors and rich fabrics that did not extinguish her striking good looks but did not call undue attention to them, either.

2. *Women who do not work want to look conservative because of the nature of their husbands' work.* I dress many wives of important men—oil executives, investment bankers, partners in major law firms, restaurateurs, advertising executives, diplomats—and their concerns are often not that different from those of women who work. If the husband's job entails great responsibility, the wife usually wants to look responsible, too. And if the husband is in a very conservative field—banking, for instance—she often feels she must look almost as conservative as he does. Like the businesswoman, she is often on display; like the businesswoman, she wants to feel confident in the correctness of her appearance.

3. *They see their clothes as an investment.* I don't have to tell you how expensive clothes are today. None of us likes to think about just how much more we pay for a pair of shoes now than we did a few years ago. Women across the country, working or nonworking, have responded to the high price of clothing by purchasing more carefully. They want clothes they can wear not just this year but next year and the year after that. They don't want to buy something so specialized that they will soon tire of it—or that other people will tire of seeing them in.

Good conservative clothing is easier to accessorize, easier to add to next year, a better investment. Conservative chic looks are not so specific that they require other pieces which will work only with them. Coordination is easier.

4. *They want their clothes to look elegant and dignified rather than trendy.* Trendy clothes can so easily look "panicky," as if you're not quite sure of who you are. Elegant and dignified clothes look as if you know *exactly* who you are.

5. *The women's movement has alerted them to the question of how sexy they want to look.* This is especially true in situations where sending a strong sexual message through their dress might undermine their goals. Women who work may be particularly concerned about this, but they're not the only ones. Many women feel that a conservative style of dress protects them from a certain amount of harassment, and it allows them to be seen more as people than as sex objects. Of course they can still be, and dress, sexy in private if they wish.

6. *They want to wear their clothes; they don't want their clothes to wear them.* Often a woman chooses a piece of clothing because she finds it beautiful to look at, but when she tries it on, something is not right—either it does nothing for her or it is so overpowering that it cancels her out.

It has always fascinated me that many artists dress unflatteringly. Their clothes are usually very interesting as individual pieces—the result of their artistic eye—but they are so taken with the clothes as objects that they don't see how these garments look on *them*.

A conservative style puts the subject—you—first. The objects—the clothes—may be beautiful and interesting, but they never overwhelm the subject.

That leads me to the other, equally important, factor in dressing well. There are many women—we've all seen them—who dress conservatively and appropriately and look absolutely terrible. Just because a garment is conservative and appropriate doesn't make it flattering. Something else has to come into play here, and that something else is chic.

Chic is a kind of artistic ability that you can develop if you learn to really look at yourself, your clothes, shapes, colors, patterns. It is the development of that ability that gives a feeling of the person inside the clothes—how things look to her, how she celebrates her own kind of beauty. In order to wield it, you must learn how shapes and colors relate to you and to each other. This is the part many women have trouble with, but it is really the most pleasurable part. I like it best, and I hope I can turn it into a pleasure for you, too.

But before I proceed into a step-by-step analysis of the particulars of conservative chic, I would like to pin down for you what it is I'm talking about and tell you what advantages it offers *you* as a style.

WHAT IS CONSERVATIVE CHIC?

Conservative chic is a way of dressing with timeless elegance in clothes that are *flattering to you* and *appropriate to your life-style.*

Conservative chic is not a dowdy, dull, matronly look, and unimaginative color combinations have no place in it. It is not a lowest-common-denominator, safe, acceptable look.

Conservative chic is not an extreme high-fashion look. What you look like is always more important than what this year's look looks like.

Conservative chic is not a preppy look. The preppy look is for kids.

Conservative chic is not a designer monogram look. Designer monograms look insecure; conservative chic is for the woman who wants to look secure in her own taste.

Conservative chic is not a "dress for success," mannish, businesslike look. It is a conservatively elegant look that can work marvelously for a woman who wants to advance in her field—or who is already at the top—but it is not a uniform of low-heeled pumps and little string ties.

Conservative chic is not a supersexy look. It's not sexless; it just doesn't make an issue out of sex.

WHERE DOES CONSERVATIVE CHIC COME FROM?

Conservative chic comes from older notions of "ladylike" dress. You can reject the negative connotations of the word "ladylike" and still accept the advantages it offers in the area of clothing: To dress like a lady used to mean to dress like a woman, but not like a sex object. And herein lies the *real* women's equivalent to the way the successful businessman dresses.

There is no point in trying to imitate the way a man dresses for work. Mannish outfits on women look wrong in every respect: They are generally unflattering, and they look stiff and self-conscious. Also, they can antagonize older men (who are often your superiors) because they violate their notions of appropriate female dress.

Even if they were right for the wrong reasons, our mothers and grandmothers had some of the answers to today's questions of how to dress. There is no need to reach into a man's closet for appropriate female business dress. What we need to emulate is the characteristics of successful male business dress; those we can adapt to our own needs.

Male business dress is very covered up—not much flesh is on display. But covered up does not mean swallowed up. The trimness in men's tailoring gives a sense of the body underneath, and the fact that men wear pants and low-heeled shoes offers them the opportunity for unfettered and unself-conscious movement. Men's business clothing is conservative, traditional—it doesn't call attention to itself. Consistent in tone and style, it also looks very "dressed," "buttoned up," and "suited up."

Old-fashioned, ladylike dress fulfilled all of these criteria, except for, sometimes, freedom of movement. Very high heels and very narrow or full skirts, for instance, do hamper freedom of movement. In general, though, what your mother wore if she aspired to be a lady was conservative, low-key, relatively covered up—"dressed." But it was feminine, too—you could see that the person wearing it was female.

I'll talk more about the particulars of women's business dress when I get to the individual garments. For now, I merely want to note that conservative chic is a direct descendant of ladylike dress, and that it is full of possibilities for a working wardrobe, or for a wardrobe that never goes to work. Conservative chic is a way to avoid sexual caricature. You don't present yourself as a male caricature (as in the mannish businesslike look) or as a female caricature (as in the supersexy look).

IS CONSERVATIVE CHIC "IN STYLE?" DOES IT GO OUT OF STYLE?

Conservative chic stands in a very special relation to fashion. It is never so *in* that it could become *out*. Expect to hear, "You look wonderful," rather than, "I love your dress." As I said, a conservative style always puts the subject—you—first. The clothes are there as an expression, an extension, of you—never vice-versa. Your clothes will subtly enhance, not overwhelm, you. Your own look and style are more important than what's "in style."

After all, barring an enormous weight gain or loss, pregnancy, severe illness, a drastic change in hair color, or extensive plastic surgery, your looks don't really change that much. *Your body shape and coloring are more or less constant. So are the shapes and colors that flatter your own shape and coloring.* Conservative chic is knowing what these are and knowing how to adapt fashion to your own ends.

WHAT IS THE SECRET OF CONSERVATIVE CHIC?

Buy clothes that are conservatively cut in chic color and pattern combinations—this book will tell you how—and build a wardrobe that looks stylish but won't go out of style.

DOWDY

CONSERVATIVE CHIC

Dress for a dignified occasion

EXTREME

CONSERVATIVE CHIC

High-fashion look

PREPPY

CONSERVATIVE CHIC

Casual look

16

MONOGRAMMED

CONSERVATIVE CHIC

Designer look

MANNISH DRESS FOR SUCCESS

CONSERVATIVE CHIC

AGGRESSIVELY SEXY

CONSERVATIVE CHIC

Pants look

CHAPTER TWO

Step One: What Are the Classics? Are They Classics for You?

When you leaf through a fashion magazine or read the copy in department store ads, you invariably come across certain styles that are referred to as "classics." Some of them are:

Clothing	Accessories
blazer	beret
cape	Chanel sling-back shoes
Chanel suit	hoop earrings
kilt	pearl earrings
pleated skirt	pumps
pleated trousers	spectator shoes
reefer coat	string of pearls
shirtdress	T-strap shoes
steamer coat	
sweater set	
trenchcoat	
turtleneck	

What the fashion media mean by a "classic" is something that has been "in style" for many years. I think it is safe to say that every item on the above list has been around for fifty years minimum—and chances are good that many will still be in style fifty years hence.

To have lasted so long, these classics must have something going for them. They do: conservative cut, line, or shape (by which I mean the kind of line that bears some relation to the actual shape of a woman's body and that is not exaggerated or extreme). While not all conservative shapes are classics, a classic is always conservative in line or cut. A classic is a conservative shape that has become famous.

The cut of a classic may vary slightly from year to year (designers perpetually strive to "update" them), but never too much. For a classic leads a kind of eternal fashion life, carrying with it the promise of appropriateness and good taste.

"Wonderful," you may be thinking. "I'll just buy only classic styles—clothes that are conservatively cut. That way I'll always have a look of timeless elegance."

When I take my first look into the closets of my clients, I often encounter this line of thinking. It's logical as far as it goes, but it doesn't go far enough. It's too formularized and impersonal.

Always watch out for the general, the easy answer. You are an individual. You can't just buy any garment described as classic and expect it to do something for you: You have to determine whether or not it is a *personal* classic. Just because a store calls a garment a classic doesn't mean it will be one for you.

To be a personal classic, a classic clothing shape must complement or flatter your own shape. And not all classic cuts *will* flatter your shape. That is why a wardrobe of indiscriminately chosen classics can look frumpy and ill fitting. The quality and the timelessness are there, and more likely than not the clothes are appropriate, but there is no sense of the body underneath them, no flattery to the wearer, no selectivity in the choice.

It can be very exasperating to find a piece of clothing that is beautiful, classic, well made, and of fine quality material, only to find that it looks awful on you. Or, maybe it doesn't look awful . . . it just does nothing for you. Unfortunately, when faced with a beautiful classic garment that seems to have so much going for it, many women turn away from that small inner voice that tells them something is wrong. They shouldn't—and you shouldn't—because unless a classic is a personal classic, it is a poor choice and a waste of money.

A personal classic, then, complements or flatters your shape. So you won't be able to choose one (unless by happy accident) until you understand your own shape. And women who know something about their shapes are in the minority. To a truly remarkable degree, modesty, fantasies, mothers' opinions, friends' and lovers' opinions, hopes, and fears influence the way most women see their bodies. (Maybe not so remarkable if you take into consideration the extent to which our society values a woman's looks over all her other qualities, even in these semi-enlightened times.)

Most of us don't know what we look like, and that's a problem for those of us who aspire to dress well. So put aside modesty and all those other notions (you'd be surprised how many of my new clients hide in their bathrooms when changing clothes—until I tell them I can't possibly shop for them without seeing what they look like) and take a good look at how you are shaped. While you needn't take off every stitch of clothing, as all those magazine articles exhort you to do, you shouldn't wear more than underwear or a bathing suit; and a full-length mirror is a must.

Without criticizing yourself, look carefully at your body, front, side, and back. Describe in detail what you see. Let me give you an example of what I mean by detail: If you look at yourself, front, side, and back, in a full-length mirror and come up with "big hips," you are not giving yourself adequate information with which to select complementary clothing. If you don't know just where, in the hip area, that bigness lies, you will continue to think and dress according to a meaningless generalization.

Big hips could mean that you are broad hipped, with a flat rear. Or, it could mean you have hips of average width, with a protruding rear. Perhaps your hipbone lies so close to your waist that it gives you a boxy, "hippy" appearance, even though your hips are not broad. Perhaps your hip fullness lies at the bottom of your seat.

Do you begin to get the picture? We are all uniquely shaped. Each body has its own rhyme and reason. The woman who knows this, and who can analyze her body in this kind of detail, has the information to choose those shapes that complement her own.

Most people never think about how much the appearance of their bodies is the result of the length and width of different parts in relation to each other. It's understanding how the parts fit together—what I call my "theory of relativity"—that will enable you to assess your figure correctly. If your legs are long *in relation to* your torso, you will appear long-legged. If your arms are long *in relation to* your torso, you will appear to have long arms. You may have long legs (in relation to your torso), but they may be longer above the knee than below the knee—or vice-versa.

If you are having difficulty coming up with specific detailed information about your shape, perhaps the following list of twenty questions can help you out. Use them as a guide, but do not limit yourself to them. Write down your answers and any other pertinent observations.

1. I carry my weight mostly_____.
2. My arms are (*long, short*) in relation to my torso.
3. My legs are (*long, short*) in relation to my torso.
4. I am (*smaller, larger*) above the waist than below the waist.
5. I am relatively (*long, short*) from shoulder to waist.
6. I am relatively (*long, short*) from waist to end of seat.
7. My waist is (*wide, narrow*) in relation to my hips.
8. My hips are (*wide, narrow*) in relation to my waist.
9. I am relatively (*large-busted, small-busted*) for my frame.
10. My bust is (*high, low, medium*) in placement on my torso.
11. My hip fullness is (*high, low, from side to side, from front to back*).

12. My shoulders are *(broad, narrow)* in relation to my hips.
13. My head is rather *(small, large)* in relation to my body.
14. My upper arms are *(firm, flabby)*.
15. My midriff is *(slim, fleshy)*.
16. My stomach is *(flat, rounded, protruding)*.
17. My thighs are *(firm, flabby)*.
18. My thighs are *(wide, narrow)* in relation to my torso.
19. My thighs are *(wide, narrow)* in relation to my calves.
20. My ankles are *(wide, narrow)* in relation to my calves.

As you will note, many of the questions that compare one part of the body with another deal with parts adjacent to each other. Although these are some of the most important relationships to learn, it is not a bad idea also to take a look at long-distance relationships such as: head size to leg length, foot size to height, calf size to upper body bulk, etc. Again, the more information you can come up with, the better prepared you will be to take advantage of the material in Chapter Three, where I describe the conservative cuts and the bodies they flatter. Knowing your own shape will empower you to choose the conservative cuts that will become your personal classics.

While I am hoping you can look analytically at your body without criticizing it, I know that most women find this extremely hard to do. I have already said that the stress our society places on a woman's appearance plays a large part in this, but I would like to dwell for a moment on the specific ways in which our society reinforces her self-critical attitude.

Whether you are aware of it or not, you have grown up with the standard of female beauty of our times—just as women in other ages have grown up with theirs. It's out there, ever-changing, making life difficult for you unless you either fit it exactly or have an extremely independent point of view about your appearance. You know what it looks like today: slim to skinny, long-legged, slim-hipped, a fair amount of shoulder, and a full bosom—it's the Barbie-Doll body. Much of the criticism women heap upon their appearance comes from the fact that, consciously or unconsciously, we are constantly comparing ourselves against this standard—and coming up short. Even this might not be so bad if our worst insecurities were not corroborated by the clothes we find in the stores—most of which seem to be cut for the "ideal" figure, whether or not most women are actually shaped that way. Though the notion of one perfect body type against which all others are measured is rather irrational, especially for those of us not shaped like the ideal, a lot of effort can go into trying to find those garments that give our bodies the illusion of the ideal shape. That's what all those figure-problem articles and books are about. A lot of figures are only "problems" if you compare them with the "ideal."

You wouldn't have picked up a book like this—and I wouldn't have written it—if we weren't concerned about how to look our best, and, living in the time we do, our "best" is always influenced by this ideal. I'm not asking you to ignore the standard of beauty of our time—that probably isn't possible for either of us—but I would like you to be aware of it, and to try to keep it in some kind of perspective. Take a look at the acknowledged beauties of other eras—they look different from our own film stars and fashion models. Beauty is partly what your own age defines it to be. Your "figure problem" might have been a hallmark of beauty in another time.

Although, in my experience dressing women—extensive if not exhaustive—I have certainly seen many women whose bodies come close to the ideal shape, I have seen many more that cluster around its opposite: smaller bust and shoulders, fuller hips and thighs. It is this second kind of body that seems to me a more typical woman's shape. Of course, I cannot say just from my own experience that the smaller-topped, larger-bottomed female body predominates, but there are certainly a lot of them out there!

Just as our time features a standard of beauty that women try to fit themselves to, it also features a dominant clothing style that we all try to fit into: tailored sportswear. Tailored sportswear (most of which fits into the classic category) is what most of us buy most of the time, for most occasions. At its purest, it is not just tailored (unfrilly and fitted to the body), but man-tailored (unfrilly and cut to flatter a man's shape). And guess which women look best in man-tailored sportswear? You've got it: the broad-shouldered, slim-hipped, long-legged "ideal."

If you have the "other" kind of female body (smaller on top and larger on the bottom) and aspire to a wardrobe of tailored sportswear, you have probably experienced a lot of frustration. For that beautiful, classic, tailored blazer with the beautiful, classic, tailored, pleated skirt will not look beautiful on you. Why not? Because a blazer, being a man-tailored jacket, takes its shape from a broad shoulder and fits lightly over the waist and (narrow) hips. Its shape echoes the classic masculine V of broad shoulders and narrow hips; thus it will not look right on very narrow shoulders, very broad hips, a very tiny waist, and a very full bosom. And, if you have broad hips, a full seat, or even just a very tiny waist, you have probably noticed that pleated skirts exaggerate these attributes in the most unflattering way.

Blazers and pleated skirts are not the only classics, nor are they the only garments that are conservatively cut. But many women on whom they are unbecoming act as if they were. You needn't make that mistake. Wear a straight dirndl (a straight skirt with minimal gathers at the waist) and a shirt-jacket (an unconstructed hip-top-length boxy jacket) instead. The straight sides of the straight dirndl are a strong vertical that gives your lower body a slim look, while the minimal gathers allow room for hips, some stomach, and a fullish rear without brutally outlining them. And the shirt-jacket's unrevealing lines can blur the outline of a large bust or add bulk to a small top. Look through Chapter Three and pick the shapes that either complement your own shape or give it the illusion of the ideal, emphasizing or de-emphasizing some parts of you in relation to other parts.

A word here about creating illusions with shape. This is an art practiced by models, actresses, dancers, and others whose personal appearance is important professionally. When Mikhail Baryshnikov performs, you may or may not be conscious of the fact that he is not tall, but he gives the impression of length when he is moving. In person, he looks slightly stocky and foreshortened because he has a very developed chest and upper body for a man of his height. When he came several times to the ballet class I usually take, I had a wonderful opportunity to observe firsthand how he achieves the illusion of length onstage. He slightly exaggerates his line by leaning out instead of remaining upright in certain positions and by moving very broadly and aggressively, so that his movements have an elongated look and feel. He knows what the audience sees, and he knows how to manipulate that to his advantage.

It is very useful to know some illusionary tricks with shape, but there are a couple of pitfalls to watch out for. First, many of these tricks work better at a distance. Did you ever know anyone who took makeup lessons that stressed elaborate contouring and shading? That's just what her face looked like afterward—a lesson in contouring and shading. And any but the *most* subtle shading is so eye-catching that it overwhelms what is really pretty about a woman's face. From the stage, or in a photograph, she might look terrific, but at close range she just looks made-up.

You can run into the same problem with clothing if your whole thrust is to manipulate shapes to create an illusion of how you are shaped. If you get too far into this, your "audience" will be conscious of it, too. And an over-concern with hiding things about your shape is a negative way to construct a look. You can hide some things, but not everything, and you shouldn't hide everything, anyway. If you try to hide too much about yourself and are unsuccessful, you will look worse than you did in your natural state; and some things, like Barbra Streisand's nose, are so distinctive and individual that they should be left as they are.

How will you recognize a personal classic? Here are some guidelines, but you'll still have to keep your eyes and ears open to find your own, truly personal, answer:

1. It will be conservatively cut so that you can wear it for years. It doesn't have to be the most strictly tailored kind of sportswear, and it might not even be a "classic" in the general sense.

2. It may be a garment you always get compliments on—or compliments may be addressed to *you* when you wear it. Before you decide that a garment is a personal classic, though, make sure that the compliments are not due to the color (a subject we'll take up later on) rather than the shape. A beautiful and flattering color, especially if worn near the face, can have such a strong impact that the garment itself will receive compliments, even if its shape is unflattering.

3. It either echoes your own shape or creates the illusion that your shape is "ideal."

4. It may be a garment you always feel good in.

5. It will usually work well with the other clothes you like to wear.

Chapter Three features a compendium of conservative cuts by garment category, with notes on the kinds of bodies they flatter. You will recognize your known personal classics there, discover many new ones, and learn the hallmarks of conservative cut and shape.

Step Two: Conservative Cuts

I am always amazed when a client asks me if a particular color is "in" at the moment. To me, color is never in—or out of—style, even though lots of advertising and fashion copy would have you think so. Cut, however, is another matter.

Take a moment and picture the most out-of-style garment you can think of, or look at old photographs of yourself in clothing you would now consider dated. Now think of the same garment(s) in different colors. They'll still look out of style, because what dates a garment is not color but cut.

A friend of mine was rather young when she married, in the mid-1960s. Thinking herself very modern, she chose a white dress that was the height of fashion at the time. Needless to say, it had a miniskirt. Today, more secure in her own style and taste, she groans every time she looks at her wedding pictures. Had she borrowed her grandmother's wedding dress, she would have looked less dated.

One advantage of choosing conservative cuts is that they do not date readily—you have a better chance of enjoying the garment for its natural life, which means as long as the fabric holds up. The less money you have to spend on clothes, the more carefully you should consider this fashion fact; however, even a woman with lots of money to spend should give it plenty of consideration. Clothes are so expensive nowadays that few of us can afford to choose wardrobes without thinking of them as an investment, particularly purchases as expensive as suits or coats. But, even if your loyalty to conservative cuts springs mainly from the negative impetus of an all-too-limited clothing budget, it can yield a positive and beautiful result, just as long as you select only those conservative cuts that are personal classics and you learn how to coordinate them with each other (see Chapter Eight, Coordination and Its Dividends).

Before we break garments down into categories, a few words about cut and shape in general.

Most women pick garments that are too complicated rather than too simple in shape.

(As a matter of fact, I question whether any garment can really be too simple.) The plainest, most unadorned sweater and skirt can be given more interest by means of good-looking jewelry or some other accessory than by all the trimming and pocket flaps and buttons in the world. Simple lines are much more elegant and flattering than complicated ones, not to mention more versatile. And really good designers know this. Just as a fashion model pares down her body to minimum weight to show the beautiful architecture of her bone structure, so a good designer pares away extraneous detail in his garments. The difference between a really fine garment and a cheaper-looking one is often a matter of simplicity: The cheaper-looking one will be fancier.

Am I talking about paying more for less here? Yes and no. Often you do pay for what the designer has had the good sense to leave off the garment. But there are less expensive garments that are beautifully and simply designed, too. Whatever you have to spend, simplicity is what you are looking for.

Suppose you digest the information in this chapter, decide you agree with me about simple, conservative shapes, and over the next few years build up a wardrobe of garments that are pared down to their essentials. Then you see some magnificent piece that is much fancier and more complicated in its shape than the rest of your wardrobe. It looks great on you. Should you pass it by in the name of discipline? If you indulge, will you need four other garments to go with your indulgence?

If such a garment flatters your shape, is a becoming color, and is appropriate to your life-style, go ahead and buy it. As for needing other garments to go with it—you may not. Many intricate garments are best set off by simple background clothing. Even if your indulgent garment is part of a group of separates that are all complicated in their cut, it may look better on you with your own simpler clothing. Say you buy a wonderful jacket that is all tucks and pleats and funny angles. Unless you are a fashion model, it will probably look better on you with simple pants and a plain sweater than with the interesting-but-complicated-looking pieces it was shown with. Or, say you buy a peasant skirt with lots of tiers. Chances are good it will look better on you with a simple pullover than with the overwhelming matching peasant blouse it was displayed with.

Don't be tyrannized by how a garment is shown in the store or by what it comes with. Think of each piece individually—you don't have to buy the whole group. Adapt what you see in the stores to your own figure, life-style, wardrobe, and comfort.

Many times, nowadays, even a single garment will come with some sort of accessory; for instance, a shirt with a matching neck scarf. Don't automatically wear them together. Your shirt may be better off with another scarf (or without one); the scarf may go better with another shirt or sweater. The garments you buy should be simple in shape, but that doesn't mean you can't wear them in interesting ways. Even if you have to wear these garments pretty much in the expected ways to work, on your own time you can and should be more experimental. And this is where the fashion magazines can be most useful. Ignore the pages of extremely high-style garments and concentrate on how the magazine accessorizes the classics and the conservatively cut garments. Then adapt the most wearable ways of tying scarves, belting, layering, etc., to what you can carry.

It may not be out of place here to mention what you probably already know: Your own line and posture affect the lines of your garments. Exercise pays off!

Are there hallmarks of elegance in the garments we are about to look at, aside from simplicity of cut? Yes, there are:

1. A garment should look like what it is. No one-piece dresses that look as if they are two-piece!

---

2. Take a dim view of flaps that have no pockets or buttons that don't unbutton.

---

3. Details should be minimal and of good quality. Buttons should usually be matching, covered, or concealed by a placket—in a word, unobtrusive. Even very fine-quality decorative buttons cut down a garment's versatility. Question all pockets. Do they add anything to the line of the garment? To your line? Avoid contrasting trim in most cases.

---

4. Avoid zippers wherever possible. Nothing does less for the back of your dress than a zipper line running down it. Never buy a turtleneck with a zipper. Large zippers as detail are trendy and cut down on versatility. Shorter zippers are okay in skirts and pants, particularly if artfully concealed.

Are there any shapes that are never conservative? Yes. To name a few: puff sleeves (they look juvenile), empire waists on street-length dresses (also juvenile), bloomers (costumey), and one-shoulder dresses (eccentric).

If any terms (like placket) are unfamiliar to you, check the glossary at the end of this chapter.

Now, on to the conservative cuts.

COATS

The Steamer

Most basic of all the conservatively cut coats, the steamer looks good on most women. Year after year, variations of it appear in coat and raincoat departments, and even as outerwear jackets. Characteristically loose fitting, it has a generous armhole, sleeve, and body, and a small collar that closes at the neck. If the body of the coat comes out of a yoke, it may be very full indeed (this variation is better on a small-busted woman). Sleeves may be raglan or set-in, possibly with a buttoned tab or buckled belt near the wrist. Front buttons are simple—often concealed by a placket. Sometimes such a coat will come with a belt; if there are riders, take them off so that you can wear the coat either way. The back might have a pleat in it. This is one of the plainest coats you can find, and therein lies its beauty: It goes with everything, some version of it flatters everyone, and it won't go out of style.

The Reefer

This is the style most women think of when they think of a "classic" coat, but an awful lot of women who buy reefers shouldn't. A man-tailored, close-fitting style, the reefer looks best on a woman with substantial shoulders and slim hips. If you have narrow shoulders with rather wide hips, it will be most unflattering. The reefer is slim and usually double-breasted with notched lapels. It may have a partial belt in back (murder on a protruding rear) or possibly even a full belt. The lapels can overwhelm a woman with narrow shoulders by taking up too much of her shoulder area. Be very sure that the scale of the lapels is not too big for your shoulders and the depth of the neckline is not too deep for the length of your upper body. Very busty women may find that such lapels break or spring oddly on them instead of lying flat against the torso.

Sometimes the reefer has pocket flaps—watch out for these if your hips are wide.

The Cape

It would be hard to think of a style that has had a longer run than the cape. In its crudest form it must go back almost as far as the wheel. This is the one garment about which I can say with absolute confidence: It will never go out of style! And it looks beautiful on everyone. A cape may be just a toss of fabric or it may be fitted around the shoulders. It may or may not have arm slits, a collar, a hood. It may be held together by a tie at the neck or buttons down the

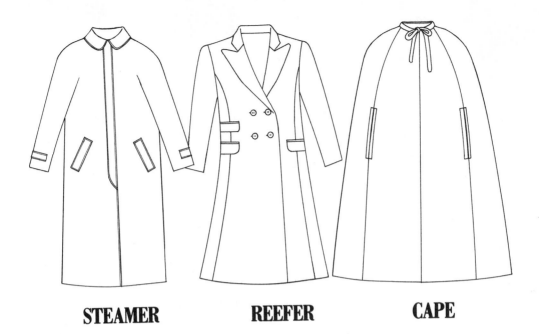

STEAMER **REEFER** **CAPE**

TRENCHCOAT **PRINCESS** **WRAP**

front (possibly concealed in a placket). Length can fall anywhere from hip to floor (longer ones are more flattering and stately). Like the steamer, the cape is a very simple style. Avoid obvious pockets, buttons, or any fussy detail.

The Trenchcoat

The trenchcoat, like the reefer, is a man-tailored style that looks best on a taller woman with substantial shoulders and slim hips. A short woman can wear a trenchcoat if she is careful to choose one that is not too overwhelming, either in the amount of fabric or the number or size of details (flaps, yokes, lapels, tabs, etc.). If you look like a package tied in the middle in a trenchcoat (and many otherwise attractive women do), choose a raincoat with a different cut. Here again, a steamer-style raincoat will look good on more women than a trenchcoat.

If a trenchcoat is *it* for you, look at the best and most expensive ones before you buy. Notice the color, cut, and kind and quality of details (like real leather buttons and buckles). Then buy the coat you can afford that comes closest to the real McCoy. If you find a good-looking well-cut trenchcoat that has poor-quality buttons and/or buckles, don't hesitate to replace them with real leather or tortoiseshell ones. They will be worth the money you invest in them. Buy a trenchcoat that is roomy and a bit on the long side—too short looks awkward . . . as if you outgrew it.

The Princess-Style Coat

This is a very feminine coat that outlines the curves of the body—the opposite of the reefer and the trenchcoat. It can look lovely on a small woman, or a woman with narrow shoulders and full hips, but it also looks nice on a taller woman who is slim and has a girlish air. The one thing you do need for it is a waist, because this is what the princess seams draw the eye to. A princess-style coat has a Peter Pan collar, a shaped bodice, a flaring skirt, and a high, tight armhole. Sleeves may puff slightly at the shoulder.

The Wrap Coat

Since the sash is what holds a wrap coat closed, don't consider one unless you look good in a belted coat. Be sure to look at the back view before you buy—if you have a protruding rear this style is not for you. Generally, a wrap coat is fairly slim with set-in, raglan, or kimono sleeves. It may have notched lapels, like a reefer, or it may have a shawl collar or mandarin or jewel neckline. It has no buttons to break up the line of the front, and the knotted sash adds a strong vertical look to the coat. If a reefer is too fitted a style for you, but you have the shoulders to carry the notched lapels, try a wrap coat with notched lapels—it is looser fitting, so it may be a little more generous toward your waist and hips. And if you have narrow shoulders, try the shawl collar version. The shawl collar or kimono wrap coat is a good choice for the woman with a smaller top and a larger bottom who wants to try to balance the two. Both add bulk and width to the upper body, making the coat skirt look slim by comparison. And the narrow shawl collar does not overwhelm narrow shoulders.

DRESSES

With so many women inclined toward suits and sportswear separates, the dress has gotten short shrift in the last few years. There haven't been enough styles to choose from, and most of what's been out there has been too girlish, frilly, or trendy. There are, however, some timelessly elegant conservative cuts in dresses, and if you don't see them one year, you probably will the next.

The Shirtdress

The obvious conservative choice in the dress area, the shirtdress is a classic, and, what's more, a classic that looks good on a variety of women. It's a natural for women who work because it coordinates so well with tailored jackets. There are so many style variations that almost anyone can find one that suits her, and it comes in a wide range of fabrics from the very casual to the very dressy.

The basic shirtdress is an elongated shirt that buttons neck to hem. It could have long or short sleeves, a pointed or small rounded shirt collar, and maybe a breast pocket. Other variations abound. You can find just about any kind of sleeve on a shirtdress: cap, dolman, puff (not conservative chic), sleeveless, etc. Some shirtdresses are cut like tents with just a buttonless placket at the neck. You can find shirtdresses with slim, full, A-line, pleated, or slit skirts. Most flattering to the majority of women is a straight, but not skinny, cut with enough fabric in it so that the skirt does not pull across the hips, and the top is roomy enough to blouse slightly above the belt.

A word here about that belt. Many shirtdresses (and many other kinds of dresses, too) come with their own matching belt or sash. Don't feel duty bound to wear the belt with the dress—it may be too monotonous looking or it may give the dress a cheaper look. A simple medium-width leather belt with covered buckle or sculptured metal buckle can transform a dull shirtdress into an elegant garment.

Don't buy a shirtdress with slits if you intend to wear it to work, and maybe even if you don't. Slits go in and out of style, can look suggestive, and, unless they are carefully finished, can make the garment look cheaply made.

The Two-Piece Dress

Before I get any further into the dress area, I want to bring up the issue of *the two-piece dress.* The shirtdress is a natural for a two-piece dress, and buying it in two pieces offers a number of advantages. First, you can choose different sizes for shirt and skirt. Secondly, you have the option of using two very basically styled pieces with a number of things in the rest of your wardrobe, especially if you buy your pieces in a fabric with some weight (it's easier to coordinate a blouse in a lightweight fabric with other pieces of different weights than it is to coordinate such a skirt). And, thirdly, with a two-piece shirtdress you can wear the shirt belted as an overblouse, offering you two advantages: An overblouse looks a little more dressed, more like a jacket than a shirt that is tucked in; and an overblouse is one of the most powerful and versatile illusionary techniques for your figure. A belted and bloused over-blouse can: add bulk to the upper body and make the lower body look narrower, conceal short-waistedness, downplay bustiness, cover and blur the line of a protruding stomach, cover midriff rolls, cover high hip fullness, soften and relax your look without appearing sloppy. In short, if you feel you have a figure problem, try it. Choose a shirt that is generously but not too voluminously cut. You want a slightly blouson look, not a huge slump of fabric.

The Dolman Dress

Few lines are more elegant and sweeping than the dolman sleeve. A dolman dress always looks dignified and it offers wonderful freedom of movement. If you have a big meeting or presentation at work and you don't want to wear a suit or a two-piece dress, a dolman dress is something you should consider. It is also a good choice for an important social event (such as speaking before a group or attending a religious service) and works wonderfully for business social occasions. The distinctive feature of a dolman dress is the dolman sleeve, which gives the top width and importance. It may have a jewel neck, a collar, or a slit neck that closes with a tie. The skirt is either quite full or straight but roomy. The dolman dress looks best belted. A cummerbund or wide wrap belt is particularly nice.

While the dolman looks great on a broad-shouldered or busty woman, it also looks good on a woman with a small top. It is very subtle in how it outlines the upper body, adding breadth and bulk to a small or small-busted

SHIRTDRESS   **TWO-PIECE DRESS**   **DOLMAN DRESS**

COATDRESS   **"BATHROBE" DRESS**   **BASIC BLOUSON DRESS**   **SWEATER DRESS**

top, softening broad shoulders, and concealing the outline of a large bust. Its problem is one of coordination—it doesn't fit well under most coats or jackets. You need a cape or a coat or jacket with a very deep armhole (like a kimono) to accommodate it.

Coatdresses and Other Wrap Styles

The coatdress is another important-looking, unfrilly dress. Sort of a dress version of the reefer coat, the coatdress has notched lapels, long or short sleeves, a double-breasted wrap front closing, and a slim skirt. It is a very close-fitting style, and it looks best in a fabric that has body and weight. Crisp and efficient-looking, the coatdress is another good choice for a working woman, or for a dignified social occasion. Because it is so fitted, you need a rather evenly proportioned figure to carry it. If you are quite busty, it may be too revealing an outline—watch out especially for the two top buttons of the double-breasted closing (you don't want them to look like two protruding nipples). Simple buttons are fine on this kind of dress. If the buttons are ornamental, be certain they really add to the look of the garment, and think about whether they may conflict with or cheapen the look of whatever jewelry you might wear. Since the coatdress is a wrap style, check to see that there is plenty of overlap in the wrap, and that the skirt closes far enough down to avoid its opening and embarrassing you.

The coatdress is a crisply tailored close-to-the-body wrap dress. Other wrap dresses are more relaxed in their line, less revealing of the body, and consequently easier to wear. I often refer to them as bathrobe dresses, because that is what their cut resembles—not a sloppy old bathrobe, but an elegant and flattering new one. A bathrobe-style wrap dress has more fabric in it than a coatdress, usually has a sash, and is the dress version of the wrap coat in the same way that the coatdress is the dress version of the reefer. It may have a shawl collar, notched lapels, or no collar, and occasionally a kimono or batwing sleeve. A wrap dress may be fine for work (particularly the shawl-collar one) if it fastens really securely (you will probably need some means other than the sash), has enough overlap, and stays closed far enough down the skirt.

The Basic Blouson

This is the least clearly defined of my dress categories. Think of it as the blouse-dress—in other words any conservatively cut dress other than a shirtdress with a bloused top. Where the shirtdress buttons up the front, the basic blouson pulls over the head or buttons in the back. This gives a beautiful, simple, uninterrupted line to the front. When such a dress has no vertical shoulder seam—it can be either an extended cap-effect shoulder or a longer sleeve that is cut in one piece with the bodice—it can be extremely flattering to narrow shoulders, giving an illusion of bulk and width to a small top. Skirts are either flared or slim but not skinny (the blouson often has an elasticized waist). This is a very simple, graceful style that marries well with interesting jewelry, belts, or other accessories. Because it is not particularly figure-revealing, it can be worn at work, and its simplicity makes it work well under jackets.

The Sweater Dress

Never wear a sweater dress to work if you are in a very conservative field, or if you have a very voluptuous or heavy figure. For a conservative chic look, a sweater dress should never cling—it should barely skim the figure. A very slender, small-breasted, slim-hipped woman might get away with a nonclingy sweater dress in a *somewhat* conservative field (but even *she* should wear a non-cling slip underneath). Sweater dresses come in many of the dress shapes already mentioned, as well as the basic collarless pullover style—just like an elongated pullover. Like other stretchy, clingy garments, sweater dresses can outline very vividly any figure disproportions or excess weight. It's better to buy them slightly too big rather than slightly too small. The right kind of underwear (noncling half or full slip, smooth and unornamented bra, briefs rather than bikini underpants) can make all the difference in your look.

JACKETS

The right jacket for you will look just as good closed as open. Don't get into the habit of buying jackets that don't fit with the rationale that you will only wear them open . . . suppose you get cold!

The length of a jacket is another feature you should give plenty of thought to. As I'll explain, most women wear jackets that are too long for them. Don't be one of them!

The Blazer

The blazer is a conservative cut, a classic, and the first style most women think of when they think of a jacket. Blazers can be single- or double-breasted, have notched lapels, and can be straight cut or quite fitted. The most traditional kind of blazer, cut like a riding jacket, has a fitted torso, a back vent, and a rather long and flaring skirtlike bottom. Most women look miserable in this style; if I had a dollar for every woman who buys this jacket and looks terrible in it, I could retire today. If you are quite tall, broad-shouldered, not too busty, and very long-legged, it is an option. If you have narrow shoulders, are busty, are short-waisted or long-waisted, have full hips or short legs, beware! These jackets are much too long for most women; they can make you look as if you are walking on your knees. Unless the jacket is perfectly fitted, the lapels strain miserably over a medium to large bosom. And the back view may be the worst of all: the vent invariably pulled open by the strain of encompassing the hips and seat, and the small of the back buckling unbecomingly because the swell of the hips does not allow it to lie flat. Most women would look better in a less fitted blazer that is shorter and has no vents.

Because the blazer is a very tailored style, it should be tailored very well, particularly if it is the fitted, traditional kind. Don't economize here. In fact, don't economize on jackets, period. With the exception of an occasional unlined, unfitted style, a jacket, more than any garment, reflects what you pay for it. Of course, you *can* buy expensive jackets that fit miserably, and you might be lucky enough to find an inexpensive jacket that fits pretty well, but in the main, jackets should be among the more expensive items in your wardrobe.

Even if you cannot spend a lot of money on a jacket, consider speaking to a good men's tailor about how a jacket should fit if you were to have one made. But when it comes to the length of the jacket, take what he says with a grain of salt. Many women look better in a jacket shorter than what a tailor would prescribe for them. I think this is because a men's tailor is used to cutting jackets for men—jackets to be worn with pants. A woman can also wear a much longer jacket with pants (which give a very long unbroken vertical line that a skirt does not). But the men's tailor has adjusted his eye to the one length—the correct length for pants.

Shorter jackets look better on most women, look better with skirts, and, the fuller the skirt, the shorter the jacket you should wear with it.

The double-breasted blazer is a much more specialized look than the single-breasted one, because, like most double-breasted garments, it looks odd when it is open. Among single-breasted blazers, the unconstructed, ventless, straight-cut, medium-length ones are the easiest to wear and the most versatile—these can often be worn belted for a change of look. If you have small shoulders and full hips, you should wear an unconstructed blazer belted and slightly bloused to bring your top in proportion with your bottom. The broad-shouldered, slim-hipped woman can wear just about any kind of blazer and, if she has long legs, just about any length.

Stay away from oversize lapels, especially if you have narrow shoulders. Buttons should be good quality and unobtrusive.

The Shawl-Collar Jacket

Many of those women who rush immediately toward the blazer rack when they need a new jacket would be better served by a jacket with a shawl collar. The shawl-collar jacket comes in a variety of lengths from waist to bottom of seat. It can be single-breasted, buttonless, or wrapped and sashed. The gently curving lines of the shawl collar are becoming to almost everyone, can look more graceful and feminine than notched lapels, and, for those with narrow shoulders, the shawl takes up less shoulder space and is a less busy line than the notched lapel. Choose your shawl-collar jackets with a narrower rather than a wider collar—the narrower one is more graceful and less likely to date.

The Chanel or Cardigan-Style Jacket

This is one of the simplest, most versatile, most enduring shapes in the whole jacket panoply. The classic Chanel-shape jacket is top-of-hip length, has four patch pockets, and contrasting buttons and trim. It has no collar. But you can find other versions that end anywhere from the waist to the leg joint, do not have pockets or buttons, and have a mandarin or small round collar. A cardigan-style jacket usually has a jewel neck, but sometimes it comes with a V-neck (which is less beautiful than the classic Chanel line but does accommodate blouses with open shirt collars nicely); sometimes it has a mandarin neck with a kimono sleeve. It is always square and unshaped in the body, and the longer versions sometimes look good belted and bloused.

The true Chanel shape is particularly flattering to women with narrow shoulders or small busts; because the front is cut so flat, it is not a good choice for very busty women—there is simply no room for a large bosom under it. If you have very broad shoulders, you may find that the simplicity of the style looks a bit unrelieved—you may look better in a jacket with a collar or lapels that break up your shoulder line. But it is the very starkness of the shape that makes it so versatile. You can always soften the neckline with a scarf, or wear a wonderful necklace or an interesting pin. It can be worn to work in a law office as part of a suit, to the theater over a camisole, or to brunch over a turtleneck and a pair of pants.

The Shirt-Jacket

Shirt-jackets look good on almost anyone, provided they are loose enough to look roomy, but not so loose that they look sloppy or overwhelming. Look carefully at the details. Do you really want or need pockets? Is the collar too large (it is more often too large than too small)? Would you be better off with

BLAZER   **SHAWL-COLLAR
                      JACKET**   **CHANEL OR CARDIGAN-
                                          STYLE JACKET**

SHIRT-JACKET   **DRESSMAKER
                       JACKET**   **BLOUSE-JACKET**

shirttails or with a straight bottom? Do you prefer a yoke?

Watch out for the more man-tailored safari styles unless you are tall and broad-shouldered. All those pockets, flaps, buttons, and epaulets look great on a fashion model; you might be better off without them. A shirt-jacket may be worn belted or unbelted—consider buying yours long enough so that you can wear it both ways. Just as pockets and flaps are too much on some women, so are shirttails often too busy a line—and without shirttails the jacket can look a little dressier.

While a shirt-jacket appears to be the most casual of jacket styles, in a dressy fabric (and sometimes even in a daytime fabric but over a garment in a dressy fabric), it can look casually dressed up in an understated and beautiful way. But it does not look right in a very conservative line of work.

The Dressmaker Jacket

The dressmaker jacket is a feminine and ladylike style that is semi- to very fitted and flares below the waist. It is usually worn by itself, without a blouse or sweater underneath. If the shirt-jacket is the most casual conservative jacket shape, the dressmaker jacket is the dressiest. This makes it most appropriate for business social events or anything in your personal social life that calls for a dignified, covered-up look. It is flattering to a woman with narrow shoulders or a small bust, but a larger-busted woman may be able to wear one if it is semi- (rather than closely) fitted. Sometimes a very broad-shouldered woman with a small bust will look good in one, but a very long-waisted woman will not, because it calls attention to her long midriff.

The dressmaker jacket usually has a shawl collar or notched lapels, but you may find other variations, such as a double-breasted style with jewel neck. If it looks right on you, and the neck is not too low, it is appropriate in a conservative office.

The Blouse-Jacket

Closely related to the dressmaker jacket is another garment that I call, for want of a better term, the blouse-jacket. This strange-sounding hybrid can be one of the most useful items in your wardrobe. Heavier than many blouses and lighter than many jackets, the blouse-jacket can be worn on its own like the dressmaker. It can look more serious than a dress and more relaxed than a suit. Like a jacket, it is worn over (rather than tucked into) a skirt (or pair of pants), and it is usually in a contrasting color (in a matching color, it could look like the top of a two-piece dress). Summer blouse-jackets are often made of linen; a winter one might be a silk with some body or a lightweight wool.

SKIRTS

The Straight Skirt

The true straight skirt—one without any gathers at the waist—has a lovely, slender line, but it can be a mercilessly revealing garment. If you have a very large difference between your waist and hips, it may not look good on you, even if you are quite slim—likewise if you have large thighs or a somewhat protruding seat. The straight skirt looks best on a slender woman who does not have a big difference between waist and hips, or a protruding rear, or on a heavier woman if she carries her weight very evenly (she can be quite fleshy, but must not have a protruding stomach, seat, or thighs). A slender woman with hipbones set very close to her waist often wears straight skirts well (she should try one without a waistband for ultimate flattery).

Never buy this style too snug, as ugly creases will develop in the groin area. To allow for unfettered movement, your straight skirt may require a kick pleat in front or back, or a front or back slit—the back kick pleat or slit is less obtrusive. Deeply slit skirts look suggestive, dressy, or trendy—they are not conservatively cut.

The A-Line Skirt

The A-line skirt has a reputation for flattering women with extra weight in the hips and thighs, but this reputation is not always deserved. An A-line skirt with no waist gathers can actually be quite revealing of the hip-stomach-thigh area, calling attention to and even emphasizing the very features you may wish to camouflage. And if you have a protruding seat and the skirt zips in back, check the back view to make sure there is no buckling over the small of the back.

There is something unsophisticated about the look of an A-line skirt that makes it more appropriate for casual wear (it makes a good jeans skirt) than for work or major social occasions.

The Dirndl

Many women who carry extra weight below the waist shy away from gathered waists, feeling that the extra fullness makes them look heavier. But strategically placed gathers at the waist are one of the most versatile and effective means of camouflaging figure problems. Waist gathers can do for the bottom half of the body what the overblouse does for the top (see the two-piece dress), provided you know how much gathering you can carry and where these gathers should be concentrated. A tightly gathered waist can be fat-making—and can give a skirt a costumey look—but a slightly gathered waist is becoming to most women.

If you sew or if you ever have a skirt made for you, experiment with those gathers by pushing them around to see where they look best. Most women look better with less fullness at the sides—it is side fullness that makes you look broader in the hips, and it can be particularly unflattering if your hipbone is placed very close to your waist. Gathers in the center-front look nice on almost everyone, and can go far toward camouflaging a less-than-flat stomach, provided the waistband is not too tight. A few center-back gathers can soften the line of a protruding or too-flat rear. Some women look better with no gathers in back and soft gathers at center-front. Even if you don't sew or have clothes made, you can make it your business to try on the different gathered varieties and decide which combination looks best on you.

The true dirndl is a tightly gathered style more suited to a dressy or ethnic look and hard for most women to wear. The more gently gathered version is easier to wear. Most flattering is what I call the straight dirndl—a slim, straight outline with just enough gathers to ease the line over hips and stomach. This style is often flattering to a woman with rather heavy hips, stomach, or thighs. It has a great deal of the appeal of the true straight skirt but is easier and more comfortable to wear.

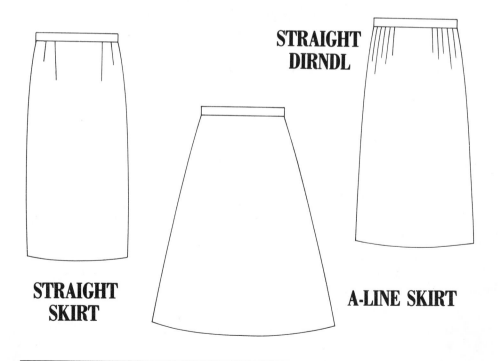

STRAIGHT DIRNDL

STRAIGHT SKIRT

A-LINE SKIRT

WRAP SKIRT **PLEATED SKIRT**

CIRCULAR SKIRT

The Wrap Skirt

Wrap skirts can have the silhouette of the straight, A-line, dirndl, or straight dirndl, or they can be pleated. The straighter styles are more elegant—fuller wrap skirts tend to look juvenile. And a skirt can wrap in front or in back.

The problem with a wrap skirt is always coverage: Is there enough of an overlap to allow you to move through the day without exposing yourself? If you work, you'll want to give this aspect special consideration. And if your waist is much smaller than your hips, you may find it difficult to come up with a wrap style that fits you in both places—the overlap may be ample at the waist but inadequate over the hips and thighs.

Even if the line of a wrap style is perfect on you, it tends to lose its shape faster than a skirt that is sewn together. And the wrap closing is an additional strong line to contend with when you choose coordinates. For these reasons, it is not the most basic of styles; there are better choices if you are looking for versatility and long wear.

The Circular Skirt

Circular skirts look best when made out of lighter-weight fabrics because they fall more gracefully over the hips that way. Most becoming to a woman with a small waist, they should not be worn too short or they will look chunky instead of graceful.

The Pleated Skirt

Pleated skirts, on the other hand, look best on women who do not have a large difference between waist and hips, because the pleats fall straighter on such a figure. There are many different varieties, and, even if pleated skirts in general are not that flattering to you, you may be able to find a style with just a few pleats that is wearable.

Pleats that are not sewn down can be a flattering choice for women with very flat rears—both regular-width pleats and knife pleats. Sewn-down pleats and kilts are easier for most women to wear, but be certain that the pleats do not open at a point that emphasizes hip fullness or heavy thighs; and, if pleats are sewn down in front, a flat stomach is a must. Very wide pleats are difficult to wear—I'm never exactly sure why. They usually look best on a tall woman.

PANTS

Trousers (Pleated Pants)

Some women do not look good in trousers—pants with pleats in front—but the majority of women will find them much more flattering than unpleated pants. Because they have a bit more fabric in them than plain pants, they give a less revealing outline to the thigh and stomach area. They are also more dressed looking than unpleated pants of the same fabric. (If you work in a field where you can wear pants, trousers will look more businesslike than plain pants.)

Of course, there are some women who should not wear pants at all in public. If you are very heavy in the hips, stomach, and thighs, give this some thought, even though nowadays "everybody" wears them. Everybody does not look good in them.

Perhaps you feel you are one of those women who cannot wear trousers successfully. Before you come to such a conclusion, make sure that you try on many pleated styles by various makers, and that you experiment with different kinds of pleats. There are single pleats and double pleats, pleats that face in toward the stomach and pleats that face out toward the hips, pleats that open freely and pleats that are sewn down (and some release lower than others). A switch in any of these areas can make a big difference in line and fit. Women who truly do not look good in any pleated pants generally have a long waist, low rear, and thighs that protrude from the hip.

Pants (Unpleated)

Leg width and length of rise (the distance between crotch and waist) are the two crucial factors in unpleated pants. A short rise on an average- to long-seated woman is ill-fitting and uncomfortable, while pants that have too long a rise for you may bag in the seat or wrinkle just below the waist.

A woman with a large difference between waist and hips may find trousers more flattering than unpleated pants.

Jeans

The jeans cut can be a classic—when worn under the appropriate circumstances (think long and hard about wearing them to work, even if there is no dress code that prohibits them). I am not talking about baggies or other jeans exotica, but about some variation of the traditional jeans cut. If you have the figure for them, jeans should fit—jeans you have to lie down to zip do not fit; they are too tight. While traditionally cut jeans that fit are not a problem to find anymore, they still look better on women who do not have a large difference between waist and hips, just like unpleated pants.

Culottes

Culottes are very much in fashion some years, impossible to find in others—but they never actually go out of style. I would not consider them part of a business suit, no matter what the fashion magazines say or the stores are showing; but they are a comfortable and flattering alternative to pants and skirts for casual wear or for dressier occasions that have nothing to do with work. Many women who look awful in every other kind of pants will look nice in culottes because they appear so much like skirts. The basic culottes style is flat in back with unpressed pleats in front. If you buy them too short, they can make you look wider; too long can look droopy or costumey. Experiment with just below the knee to midcalf to find the best point for you.

Women who have small waists and quite large hips usually wear culottes successfully, but they also look good on straighter figures.

BLOUSES

The Shirt

A classic that looks good on just about everyone, the shirt is what most women

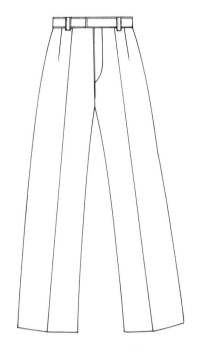

TROUSERS (PLEATED PANTS)

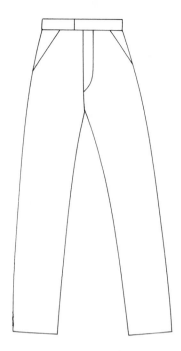

PANTS

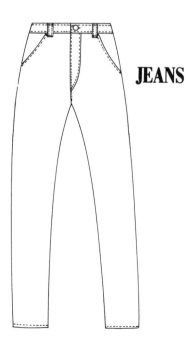

JEANS

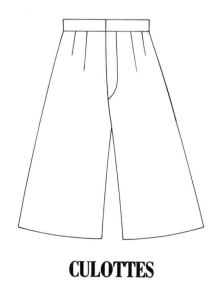

CULOTTES

think of when contemplating the blouse category. If you want your shirt to remain a classic, choose one that is not fitted in the body, has a collar on the small side (no long, droopy points), has simple, covered, or concealed buttons down the front, and has no little triangles cut out of the cuff edge to give it "interest." A straight-cut, unfitted shirt has a more relaxed look than a very fitted one—and it doesn't have to be perfectly tucked in to have a good line. Loose-fitting shirts can also soften the outline of a large bust or add width to a small top. Be wary of shirttails; if you decide to wear your shirt belted as an overblouse they can look funny, especially if they are deeply cut—a straight edge is more versatile.

Some things you might consider are whether you want a shirt to button to the neck, in which case it will probably have a stand collar, or whether you prefer an open notched collar without a stand. I often find I like the look of a collar without a stand—it can be dressier, a little more elegant than a stand collar, which is more of a sportswear look. If you like a very casual, sporty look—and if you like to lift the back of your shirt collar—a stand collar has the body to accomplish that. And if you want to open your shirt neck and wear the collar outside your jacket, you may need the stand to allow room for it to fit over a thicker jacket collar.

A shirt can have a pointed or rounded collar, or just a band without a collar, and a variety of sleeves: long, short, cap, three-quarter, raglan, etc. It may or may not have a yoke. Watch out for yokes if you are very round-shouldered—they can emphasize that curve.

A shirt can be very detailed: For instance, a safari shirt may have all kinds of buttons, tabs, pockets, flaps—great if you are tall and broad-shouldered. Or it can be extremely simple—a notch-collar style with no pockets, concealed buttons in a placket in front, and covered buttons at the wrists.

The more casually you wear your shirt, the more you can play with how you wear it. Try turning up the collar at the back, rolling the sleeves, knotting the bottom at the waist, wearing one shirt over another (for example, a loosely cut shirt over a turtleneck or T-shirt), filling in the neck with a scarf or wrapping one under the collar. Don't just put it on; wear it.

The Tie-Neck Blouse

Feminine without being frilly, the tie-neck blouse can soften a very tailored suit or pair graciously with trousers or a skirt with some gathers. Cut loose in the body and usually long-sleeved, it can have little string ties or wider ties that make a soft bow. The latter is more versatile because you can loop the ties into a bow or an ascot, or wrap them various ways for a number of different looks.

SHIRT

TIE-NECK BLOUSE

SHAWL-COLLAR BLOUSE

PEASANT BLOUSE

BACK-CLOSING BLOUSE

If you are extremely busty, the tie-neck blouse may be too overwhelming on you; likewise if you are very tall and long-waisted. Otherwise, it is a style that flatters a large number of women.

The Shawl-Collar Blouse

Like the shawl-collar jacket, the shawl-collar blouse has a line that is very flattering to most women. Choose a narrower rather than a wider shawl collar, especially if you have very narrow shoulders or are very small on top. A surplice-wrap blouse with shawl collar is a very good choice for a busty woman: The strong diagonal line seems to draw the eye away from the horizontal quality of a full bust.

The Peasant Blouse

Like culottes, the peasant blouse has been around for many years, but it tends to be a somewhat faddish style. For that reason, you will get more out of it if you restrict it to the more casual or dressy fringes of your wardrobe. The peasant blouse comes with necklines of varying depth. Its soft, flowing lines should never be broken by a zipper (the lower-neck ones pull over the head; higher-neck styles should have a slit with button, hook, or tie closing). Sleeves are always full and can be elbow length or long—short can make you look kittenish. A peasant blouse is not a conservative choice for work, and is to be avoided if you are very short-waisted, because it could give you a slightly dumpy look.

Back-Closing and Pull-On Blouses with Various Necklines

More than any other garments we have looked at, blouses come in a great many varieties, especially when it come to necklines. Unless you are buying a blouse for a very serious purpose—an interview, a dignified social occasion (business or personal)—you have a little more leeway in choosing the cut of your blouses than other garments, while still maintaining a conservative cut. Then, too, blouses can be less expensive than skirts, jackets, and coats, so a nod toward the style of the moment, unless it is really faddish, is not the investment it might be in other areas. So that you may take advantage of this opportunity, I want to call your attention to some of these different shapes and to the fact that this is an area where you can build variety into a very basic wardrobe.

Many women think of blouses, and especially shirts, as buttoning up the front—and most of them do. However, a back-button blouse may be a better look for you for a number of reasons. If you are a woman who is narrow in the shoulders or very small on top, a back-button blouse can give you a broad, uninterrupted expanse in front that adds width to the top and can help balance fuller hips and thighs. There is something very pure and elegant about the unbroken line of such a blouse, and it gives you the opportunity to accessorize more freely with earrings, necklaces, pins, and scarves. Because you don't have to take buttons into account, you can select more interesting accessories that can be concentrated around your face, where they may do the most for you. Back-button blouses come with boat necks, jewel necks, square necks, V-necks, and mandarin collars (to name a few), as well as many different sleeve lengths. If you are small on top and have upper arms that are in good shape, consider blouses with extended shoulders for summer. Very busty women should consider V-neck styles to avoid an overstuffed look, and they can worry less about gapping between buttons if the buttons are in back.

A pull-on blouse could be something like a silk sweatshirt—slightly blouson with no buttons front or back (and no zipper, obviously), so the eye can focus completely on the neckline.

A word about necklines in general. Necklines are often spoken about in relation to the shape of the face and the length of the neck. But your neck is also connected to the rest of your body. Consider face shape and neck length, but also think about shoulder width and the relation of what is above to what is below the waist.

What about necklines for work? Many women who work in conservative fields feel that their only choice is a shirt that buttons to the neck with a little tie. I seriously question this. When a man wears such a combination, it is a very closed-up look at the broadest and most expansive part of his anatomy. For a woman, this is often not the case. A woman with narrow shoulders who is smaller on top and bigger in the hips will have a very choked-up uptight look in this getup. She needs a more expansive look at the neck and is better off with an open collar. And when a very busty woman wears a closed-up, tied-up neckline, she often looks stuffed into her clothes.

Before you buy this style, take a really serious look at yourself in it—there are other options.

SWEATERS

Sweaters are not appropriate attire if you work in a conservative field, and they are not a good bet for work in *any* field if you are very heavy or busty. If you have a larger bottom than top, a fairly heavy, somewhat loose sweater worn over a skirt or pants will help balance your silhouette. Avoid ribbing, except around sweater edges—it brings anything you might want to downplay into sharp relief.

The Turtleneck

A turtleneck that is not too fitted is a classic that looks good on almost everyone. Never, never buy one with a zipper. The beauty of the turtleneck is the soft, unbroken roll of the collar, and a zipper brutally destroys this. If you are afraid a turtleneck will mess your hair or makeup, tie a scarf over your head and face before you put it on, or buy one of those zip-front, net hair and makeup protectors.

Women with short necks and heavy faces can wear turtlenecks, too. Don't bother with the mock-turtle; the real turtle is much more graceful.

Cowl necks are another story. They are much harder to wear because they take up more room in the neck and shoulder area and have a busier and more overwhelming look. Don't buy a cowl-neck sweater if you have very narrow shoulders—it may overpower you.

The Jewel-Neck Pullover

Many older women dislike the neckline of the traditional jewel-neck pullover. They feel it draws attention to a neck that is rapidly losing its tone. Sometimes this is true; but the jewel-neck pullover is such a wonderfully simple shape that it lends itself to all kinds of interesting accessorizing that can camouflage such a problem. So, don't disqualify it unless you dislike wearing scarves or jewelry at the neckline.

A jewel-neck Shetland sweater worn with a shirt underneath is a preppy look; it is not conservatively chic on a grown woman. This is *not* a way to camouflage an aging neck. You will look older rather than younger if you try it.

The jewel-neck pullover is not a good choice for a very busty woman, who will invariably look better in a more open-neck style.

The V-Neck Pullover

This style looks very flattering on a busty, broad-shouldered woman, and miserable on a woman with narrow shoulders. You can be broad-shouldered and small-busted and wear it, too.

The V-neckline is harder to combine gracefully with jackets than the turtleneck or the pullover.

TURTLENECK

JEWEL-NECK PULLOVER

V-NECK PULLOVER

CARDIGAN

SWEATER-JACKET

The Cardigan

The cardigan can range anywhere from the classic matching-sweater-set variety in a plain, flat wool, cashmere, or cotton to a thickly textured garment that looks like any of the jacket shapes we have already covered. As a matter of fact, a sweater-jacket is the third wonderful hybrid garment I would like to point out to you (along with the aforementioned shirt-jacket and blouse-jacket). A sweater cut like a jacket is an opportunity to wear a jacket in a more relaxed way.

Traditional cardigans either button up to a round neck or a shallow V-neck (a good line if you wear open shirt collars). They may or may not have pockets. Length is very important here—the longer ones look better on tall, long-legged, slim-hipped women; the shorter ones are preferable for most women. Of course, you can buy a cardigan on the long side and wear it that way with pants, then belt and blouse it to a shorter length for skirts (be certain pockets will not interfere with this).

The Sweater-Jacket

Sweater-jackets look good as blazers (squarely shaped), shawl-collar styles, buttonless cardigans, and shirt styles. They will, however, tend to lose their shape faster than a true jacket.

Although my purpose in enumerating and describing the conservative cuts has been to narrow down the field so that you can avoid shapes that date readily and do not flatter you, I think you can see that there is still a great deal to choose from. I hope you have found shapes that would ordinarily have escaped your attention—some of them might become your new personal classics!

SOME CLOTHING SHAPE TERMS

Collars and Necklines

jewel—high, round, collarless neck
mandarin—standing, broken-band collar
mock-turtle—standing collar that does not roll over
shawl—narrow, curved, unbroken lapels
stand—little band stitched between the shirt
    neckline and the collar that makes the
    collar appear to stand up on the neck
surplice-wrap—diagonal front–overlap neckline

Sleeves

batwing—deep armhole sleeve that is a little shallower than the dolman
cap—just covering the top of the shoulder
dolman—cut as part of the bodice, with a deep armhole that
    extends almost to the waist
extended shoulder—like a seamless cap sleeve
kimono—unshirred, wide, deep armhole sleeve
puff—short sleeve gathered at the shoulder and sometimes at the end
raglan—set into the neckline by a seam that slants to the underarm
set-in—seamed to a vertical armhole

Miscellaneous

cummerbund—wide, horizontally pleated belt that closes at the back
placket—overlapping strip of fabric that conceals a zipper or buttons
princess seams—long verticals that shape the torso to either side of center-
    front and center-back
rise—the distance between crotch and waist in pants
yoke—fitted shoulder piece into which the body may be shirred or pleated

Your Own Coloring

Certain colors will look wonderful on you, some will look terrible, and others will look neither. It depends upon how they agree with your own coloring. If that heavenly shade of green that you are so drawn to makes you look like death warmed over, this is why. Your skin tone, hair color, and the color of your eyes largely determine what colors will look best on you, and a change in any of them (a summer tan, change of hair color, tinted contact lenses) can upset the balance of what used to work.

If you are dying to wear a color that you know is not becoming to you, by all means don't wear it near your face. The farther away from your face, the less you need to concern yourself with whether or not a color is a personal classic; thus you can feel freer with a skirt or a pair of shoes than with a blouse, scarf, or sweater.

What about all those color theories that people are talking about? Do they work? The ones I have seen offer answers that seem to me too general to work for the individual. If you try one, be critical of the results. Do the colors really look best on you, or are you just feeling relieved that someone else has made the choice?

My own approach to color is a combination of intuitive and hands-on, so it is possible that I have a natural bias against such an approach. I like to look at a new client in the clothes she already owns; then I experiment with whatever other colors she and I have available to arrive at the best shades for her. (You can do this, too, with whatever you already have in your closet, paying special attention to how colors look near your face.) I never make up my mind about a woman's best colors when she opens the door to greet me, because, in my experience, there is no substitute for trial and error if you want a truly individual look.

There are, of course, certain colors that look good on the vast majority of women (I will get to them later on in this chapter), but that is a generalization, too. Try them, but reserve judgment. You are not the vast majority of women.

Lighting and the Time of Day

Colors change in different kinds of light. Fluorescent light, particularly, has a ghastly and draining effect on color. It is always wise (although not always practical) to look at yourself in a color in the kind of lighting situation you will be in when you wear it. If this is too difficult (and it often is for most of us), at least start to notice how the colors you wear hold up in different kinds of light.

I am most forcefully reminded of the lighting factor whenever I get as a new client a young woman who has gone to school in a countrified setting, where there is lots of natural daylight, and who is now training for a position in a New York office. Many of these women have gotten used to wearing little or no makeup—they really didn't need much in their prior setting—but to wear no makeup in any large, fast-paced city is to look washed-out and even enervated unless your own coloring is very vivid indeed. In a big city, you usually work in a tall building, and a lot of tall buildings means very little natural light. Then, too, the fast pace of big-city life demands a more sharply etched impression than a more relaxed country setting. If you are such a young woman, I sympathize with your preference for the natural look, but you must come up with some kind of compromise unless you want to become a victim of fluorescent fade.

Your Personality

Personality affects the way a color is perceived on you. If you look best in strong colors and you have a very strong personality, the combination may be too much in some instances. Other people may find you overwhelming. Of course, there are times when that effect may be just what you want, but a delicate business or social situation requires special consideration. You may be better off picking colors that are becoming but less striking than your best ones.

Or, you might be a very shy, quiet person, but your particular coloring is most complemented by very strong colors. The contradiction between what you wear and how you behave may come across stronger than anything else about you. And that would be a mistake. In some circumstances you, too, might be better off in colors that are second-best but do not overwhelm you.

The Other Colors You Are Wearing

The same color can look very different depending on the colors you place next to it. You may have seen some very good examples of this on those placemats some restaurants use to keep the kids occupied until the food comes. Because of this phenomenon, certain colors will look good in some combinations and not in others. And a color you detest may be just the right accent in a print—the catalyst that pulls all the other colors together.

Texture

Some people can wear certain colors in some textures and not in others. The best example is black. There are women who look awful in black wool flannel or black matte jersey, but they can carry off black velvet or black taffeta (more about this at the end of the chapter).

Tendency to Soil

Wearing a very pale color in surroundings where you are bound to get soiled is a bad bet no matter how becoming it is to you, for the dirt will always be more visible than the color.

Notions of Etiquette

A color may look great on you, but it may be perceived as inappropriate for the occasion. A white dress is not the thing to wear to someone else's wedding (neither is a black one, still, according to many people), no matter how smashing you look in it, unless you are out to get the bride's goat. A chartreuse suit will not go over well in investment banking. And, while nowadays you needn't wear black to a funeral, good taste still dictates that you wear something subdued in color.

Color does not exist in a social vacuum. People still have feelings about color appropriateness.

Regional Differences

Certain colors look more appropriate in some parts of the country (or the world) than others. Take a look at what the well-dressed natives wear. In New York, dark colors in summer are considered chic; in California and Florida, lighter colors prevail. Very vivid colors may look great on you in a tropical setting, but may seem like too much back home—and not just because you have lost your tan.

I think you can see why I feel that choosing colors for yourself is not the simple undertaking proclaimed by some color theorists. There are a lot of factors to consider and it will, and should, take time to come up with the right answers. If you are having trouble with colors not working for you, run down the list and see if any of the factors I have mentioned could be causing the problem.

COLOR COMBINATIONS

Perhaps the colors you are choosing for yourself are flattering and appropriate but your combinations are not very interesting.

This is a very common problem. For many women, the idea of a multicolor combination begins and ends with red, white, and blue: patriotic, but boring. Other combinations that look tried and true to many of us are:

navy with red	tan with white
navy with gray	royal blue with bright green
pink with light blue	charcoal gray with light gray
hot pink with bright green	combinations of primary colors
green with yellow	combinations of pastels

There is no rule against wearing such combinations, but they are what one all too often sees—and many of them are combinations of colors that are hard for most women to wear. If you are restricting your thinking to one group of colors, such as primaries, remind yourself that the spectrum also includes pastels, neutrals (such as tan and gray), and many wonderful and exciting colors that are neither primaries, neutrals, nor pastels, but what I call off-shades—such as burgundy, rust, celadon (a pale, grayish green), taupe, grayish lavender, and luggage (an orangey brown).

If you have been getting in a rut with tried and true combinations, experiment with some of the following:

medium brown with medium blue	mauve with luggage
dark brown with dark purple	taupe with blue-gray
olive green with red	camel with olive green
beige with dull green	cordovan (brown that is almost
burgundy with forest green	burgundy) with red
burgundy with apricot	cordovan with celadon
mauve with taupe	taupe with bright blue
black with pale green	rust with dark gray

Past association with certain colors may be what is holding you back. If your mother told you blue was your color, you may be reaching for it without really seeing it anymore. Maybe blue isn't your color, and even if it is, maybe it's not the blue you've been choosing. Perhaps your best friend looks wonderful in red, and you have been wearing red hoping to produce the same effect—but different people arrive at the same ends by different means.

Picture for a moment a serviceable, classic, dark brown suit with a deep purple blouse. Or a beige suit with a dull green blouse instead of your usual white or cream. Imagine a pair of tailored burgundy pants with a simple apricot lambswool pullover—the color adds immediate interest. Think of a taupe pantsuit with a silky mauve blouse, a bright blue flannel shirt, a blue-gray turtleneck. Or a cordovan reefer with a bright red scarf.

Many people pick primary colors to wear because they see them as "happy colors"; but primary colors are hard for most women to wear. Off-shades are easier. Others pick navy because it's safe (dark enough not to show soil, more ladylike than black, supposedly goes with everything, has a "classic" reputation), or black because it's supposed to be sexy. But navy is one of the hardest colors to wear, and black, to be flattering, may require a very special makeup that the wearer is not up to bothering with. Question yourself about the colors you have chosen. And don't let the reputation of certain colors sway you.

As a teenager, I had my own problems with color connotations. In bed with the flu and running quite a temperature, I read a passage in a Russian novel where the character wore a pair of lavender gloves that were described as very elegant. For years afterward, I was drawn to every lavender dress and blouse and skirt I came across, and I bought several pieces in that color. Unfortunately, lavender, especially all by itself, doesn't look that great on me. I was dimly aware of this, but every time I put on a lavender garment, the quasi-hallucinatory lavender gloves superimposed themselves on my offending image. There was something so romantic about the idea of them, that it overwhelmed my already quite developed color sense.

Perhaps you have had a similar experience. Try to set emotional factors aside and really *see* colors, both on yourself and in combination with each other.

Some women get all hung up on the figure-correcting properties of color. Color can minimize some figure problems—to a point. If you look at color solely in terms of figure correction, you are making a big mistake: You are losing an opportunity to flatter yourself with the colors that are most becoming to you, and you will only "correct" your figure to a limited degree. Color should not be *only* remedial. While it is true that dark skirts and pants look better on heavy hips and thighs, and that contrasting horizontal stripes can be broadening, don't concentrate only on the negative. Use color positively—especially around your face.

Watch out for a tendency to match colors up too neatly. If you are at a point where you are struggling to get two colors to work together, this is a difficult concept to understand. But things can match *too* well; sometimes one color that is a little off can give an outfit a certain charm and individuality. Consider shoes in an unexpected shade, or a scarf that does not repeat any of the colors you are wearing. By the same token, eye shadow need not echo the color of your blouse—pick something that goes with your face first and that complements (but doesn't match) your blouse. Too matching can be too much.

Color Contrast

Another reason you may be in a rut about combining colors may be your notions about color contrast. For many women, the problem is their consistent choice of high-contrast combinations. If your concept of color combining is navy blue and white (or light gray), you are picking high-contrast combinations, which means that you see dark colors as going with light colors and vice-versa. It simply never occurs to many women that dark colors can go with dark colors, light colors can go with light colors, and medium tones can go with medium tones—all three of these are examples of low-contrast combinations.

While many women pick high-contrast combinations for themselves, most women actually look best in low-contrast combinations, which are less demanding of your own coloring (with the possible exception of combinations of dark colors, such as dark brown with dark purple). High-contrast looks can be very dramatic, but they often overwhelm the wearer; low-contrast looks are more subtle.

If the high contrast of a navy suit with a white blouse does nothing for you, experiment with combining two colors of a similar depth or darkness. Try the navy suit with a burgundy blouse, a light-gray suit with a tan blouse, a medium-brown suit with a red blouse—all low-contrast combinations. Such combinations can have a richness that sharper contrasts lack. And a mixture of subtle off-shades—all of similar depth—can have a fascination all its own: Picture taupe with blue-gray, or rose, or dull green.

Sometimes you have to wear a high-contrast combination even if it is not becoming—perhaps as a uniform or because there is nothing else appropriate for a special event in your closet. Or, you may like the look of them so much that you wear them without regard to color flattery. In either case, proper makeup can help bring such an outfit into line with your own coloring—but it will probably be a makeup somewhat different (possibly stronger or more colorful) from what you usually wear.

There are "classics" in color combinations just as there are in combinations of shapes. In the high-contrast area, black with white or cream and black with tan come to mind; in the low-contrast area, tan with gray and medium blue with medium brown are what I think of first. As with classic shapes, be certain these classic color combinations are really flattering to you—don't be seduced by their reputation. And even if you *can* wear them, give some thought to how you distribute each color.

If you are a potential black with white or cream wearer, begin by discovering which looks best on you: white or cream. Are you better off with the white or cream nearest your face rather than the black? If you wear the black near your face, is your makeup adjusted for that? How much of each color should you wear, and where? What about shoes and a bag (I can tell you that you will almost always do better with black than with white here). Do you feel you need to wear equal amounts of each color? If you do, take a hard look to see if that is really flattering. Perhaps three-quarters (skirt, shoes, bag, belt) of the outfit should be black and only one-quarter (blouse) white or cream.

If black and tan is your combination, be sure to choose a tan that complements your skin tone. Check out black against your face as above. Consider how much you can wear of each, as above.

In a tan with gray combination, choose shades of each that are becoming to you. Put the most flattering one near your face; for most women, that will be the tan. You will find tan shoes and bag easier to find and more versatile than gray. Follow the same procedure for the medium brown with medium blue (the brown accessories will be easier to find and more versatile).

But whether you decide on high- or low-contrast color combinations (and some women look good in both), you don't have to wear the same old boring colors in the same old boring combinations. No matter how little you have to spend on clothes, you don't have to economize on color. You can translate color ideas from the most expensive sources into the most inexpensive garments. Do what the designers do: Go to museums and look at the work of fine painters, look at the color combinations in beautiful printed fabrics, check out the fashion magazines, go to your local paint store for paint swatches (when you get home, cut them up into separate colors and mix and match them for new ideas). The colors you wear should flatter your coloring, but there is no law against a color combination's having interest of its own.

Monochrome and Tones of the Same Color

A color combination does not need to be high-contrast, nor does it need to have *any* contrast—it is possible to wear just one shade of one color and look very elegant indeed. Does that sound boring to you? Does it remind you of bad experiences with dyed-to-match? The secret to such a look is in how you use texture, which I will have more to say about further on. If a totally monochromatic look sounds like too much of a good thing, consider one that is basically monochromatic except for the accessories. If you are a woman who looks best in the quietest, most neutral shades (such as pale tan, pale gray, white, or cream), but you enjoy strong color, reserve it for your accessories—

MONOCHROMATIC

HIGH-CONTRAST

LOW-CONTRAST

and wear them far from your face. A pale-gray skirt and sweater can look wonderful with dainty bright blue shoes and narrow belt, or shoes and handbag. Just don't have too many bright spots or the effect will be cute.

Many tones of the same color is one of the hardest color combinations to pull off. For some reason, it can easily look cheap. Don't try it unless you have a very sophisticated color sense.

"Correcting" Your Coloring

Just as many women go to great lengths to conceal figure problems by selecting shapes and colors primarily for their figure-corrective properties, so many women choose the colors they wear in the hopes of correcting what they see as problems in their coloring. Nowhere are these fears more successfully preyed upon than in the area of hair and makeup color.

The first most obvious example is all those women who go blonde because blonde is "better" than dark. It isn't. If you have dark hair and eyebrows, think a long time before going blonde. While it is often true that the older a woman gets, the softer her hair color should become, it is not always true, and a drastic shift may be most unbecoming. Not every skin tone is flattered by blonde hair. And you are committing yourself to great expense, a lot of work or upkeep time, and potential damage to the quality of your hair for very dubious results.

The second most obvious example is all the women who buy makeup foundation with lots of pink in it to "correct" a sallow or greenish complexion. Beware the advice of the makeup artist or salesperson who suggests such a course of action. Who needs a pink face with a green neck? What about the rest of you? The only thing a foundation makeup should do to correct your skin is cover blemishes or color variations—it should never change your skin color. Color should be added with blusher or rouge to the areas that need it, never to the entire face. A skin with a green or yellow cast can be just as beautiful as one with a pink or brown or ivory tinge. Work with what you've got.

Beware the hairdresser or makeup artist who gives everyone the same look, because it's "the look" of the moment or it's "prettier." That doesn't make it right for you.

In clothing, too, color should never be just a corrective. Sometimes the strongest color look you have is one that echoes your own coloring. If you are a tawny blonde with a warm skin tone and hazel eyes, you can echo your coloring in your clothes with warm tans, golds, and greens, which can give you a marvelous golden-girl look. Don't throw that away by feeling that your coloring is monotonous and has to be "picked up" all the time with, for instance, lots of red. Be open to both possibilities. And if you have an olive skin, olive green can be a wonderful color for you if your makeup includes a flattering blusher.

Colors That Look Good on Most Women

As you may recall, I mentioned at the beginning of this chapter that there are colors that look good on most women. My reason for not enumerating them at that point was not to tease you, but to give you a chance to look over the list of factors that can affect how color looks on you and, at the risk of boring you by repeating myself, to remind you that you are not most women. And here I am saying it again: Do not rush blithely out to buy clothes in these colors. Try them on, experiment, see how you look and feel in them.

Enough. The color that looks good on most women is burgundy. There are certainly many women for whom burgundy is not the *best* color, but I have never yet come across the woman on whom it did not look good. Even if nothing else in this chapter makes any sense to you—if color in general is an impossible area for you—go out and try on something in burgundy. If you have no time or energy to experiment with color, or no confidence in your eye, burgundy is as close to foolproof as you can get.

I don't know exactly why this is so; I just know it *is* so. But I can offer some possible reasons. Burgundy is a deep color with dignified associations. It is dark enough to look serious (and slimming), but it has the warmth of the red family to which it belongs. It goes with just about any color you can name (which makes it, along with its browner cousin, cordovan, the ideal choice for accessories). It is subdued enough for a ruddy complexion and pink enough to complement a green or sallow one. It looks great with all hair colors—including gray and white.

If your closet is wall-to-wall navy blue, consider a conversion to burgundy. Navy is one of the hardest colors to wear, but it is endlessly popular. Though the women who look beautiful in it are the exception rather than the rule, it carries with it, as I have already said, all those wonderful connotations of correctness and good taste. I have seen it look terrific on women with black hair and very fair skin and on some women with the warm, tawny coloring I talked about a few paragraphs back. All others should think long and hard before investing in it.

I can also tell you that blues in general are hard to wear and often unflattering to skin tones, while reds are easier. That does not mean you will be able to wear any red and no blue—shade and depth must be very carefully chosen. The two easiest blues to wear are a soft, medium blue-gray and blue-violet.

When I speak of reds, I am not just referring to true, primary red and burgundy, but also to all the soft off-shades of red: rose, mauve, nude, coral, peach, apricot, lavender. These are what I call the blusher colors, and these are the colors that look good next to most women's faces. If you have to wear a navy suit (and possibly it looks awful on you), try a blouse in one of these lovely shades. Likewise, if you have a dark gray suit that makes you look like a prison matron, try it with a blouse in mauve, apricot, or deep rose. As a matter of fact, take a long look at the shade of rouge or blusher that is most becoming to you, and find a blouse or sweater to match it; then try that blouse or sweater with everything in your wardrobe, whether you feel it "goes" or not. You will be in for some pleasant surprises.

Other colors that look good on a large number of women are tan (but the shade will vary from woman to woman) and what I call banana—a very pale shade of yellow that is almost a cream. White or cream, but often not both, also flatters lots of women.

What about colors that are hard to wear? Aside from blue there is just about every shade of yellow except banana. Gray can be very draining—especially the darker shades. Bright green is hard; olive or forest tones are easier. Black can be hard near the face, although I consider it easier than navy (a low-cut neckline can work wonders here—it moves the black farther from your face). Very dark brown can be hard, although warm, medium, reddish browns look good on lots of women. Chartreuse and orange are also difficult.

Experience has shown me that more women look good in medium tones of just about any color than in extremes of dark or light. Again, this is a generalization; this may not be you. Test it out.

PATTERN

So far, just about the only thing I have said about pattern is that a color you detest can be just the right accent in a print, and that a color is affected by the colors that surround it. I have waited to discuss patterns for a purpose—many of my clients complain about how complicated it is to combine them, how hard it is to know what colors to pull out to accessorize them, etc. They do complicate matters, although there are some ways of dealing with them that are almost foolproof—even if you think you have no idea what you are doing.

Just as I prefer to have you look at shape before thinking about color, I think it makes more sense to learn how to work with solid colors before diving into patterns. And for the truly pattern-phobic, I can offer the reassurance that you

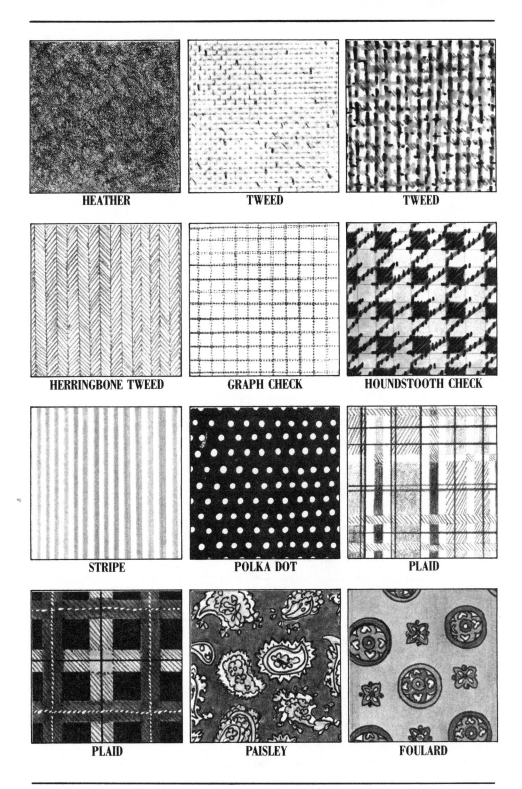

HEATHER

TWEED

TWEED

HERRINGBONE TWEED

GRAPH CHECK

HOUNDSTOOTH CHECK

STRIPE

POLKA DOT

PLAID

PLAID

PAISLEY

FOULARD

can be beautifully and elegantly dressed—and conservatively chic—and never wear a pattern or a print. If it makes you feel better, you can lead your entire life in solid colors. And if you have a very limited clothing budget, this approach sometimes makes very good sense.

However, most of us find some patterns very beautiful, would like to wear them and even combine them.

Let's begin by considering the different kinds of patterns and prints. Floral prints usually come to mind first. Then there are what I call representational prints (I think the fashion industry sometimes calls them "figurative"), which picture animate or inanimate objects other than flowers, such as, faces, tubes of lipstick, beach balls, flying geese, Eiffel towers, or what have you. There are large geometrics. And last but by no means least are the menswear patterns— tweeds, plaids, paisleys, checks, stripes, foulards (small geometrics), and heathers.

Lovely as many floral prints are, they are so stereotypically feminine that the woman who works in a conservative field should think hard before investing in them. If you feel you cannot live without an occasional floral print for work, it's better to choose a small-scale abstract floral than a large-scale realistic one—the former looks more businesslike.

Representational prints are an even worse choice for the woman who works in a conservative field. They are distracting, can look silly or cutesy, and generally detract from a professional appearance. You don't want a business superior or prospective client to focus on (a) if, or (b) why, those are scotty dogs running rampant on your blouse. Such prints can be witty and fun for a few days at a resort or for casual wear in a nonbusiness situation. Save them for such occasions.

If you want to wear a representational print for work, choose something calm and neutral like a small leaf pattern.

There is another and even better reason why floral, representational, and large geometric prints should not make up the bulk of your wardrobe (whether you work or not). You, and the people who see you in them, will tire easily of such patterns. Representational prints (and florals are representational, too) are very concrete and make a very specific impression. Because the menswear patterns are more abstract, they make a less specific impression, are more versatile, and are harder to tire of. While large geometrics are also abstract, their size makes them specific, memorable . . . and soon boring. If you like to wear patterns and you work—and/or your wardrobe budget is limited—you will be better served by the abstract menswear patterns.

But even the versatile menswear patterns can be broken down into more and

FLORAL

SMALL GEOMETRIC

SUBTLE REPRESENTATIONAL

FLORAL

SMALL GEOMETRIC

SUBTLE REPRESENTATIONAL

ABSTRACT FLORAL

LARGE GEOMETRIC

REPRESENTATIONAL

LARGE FLORAL

LARGE GEOMETRIC

LARGE REPRESENTATIONAL

less difficult to wear. Easiest to wear are the small-gauge patterns that are closest to solids: small, quiet-colored, low-contrast heathers and tweeds. Large, color-contrast plaids and wide stripes are the most difficult. A tiny, low-contrast check in muted colors is easy to wear; a huge black-and-white houndstooth check is much more difficult.

Even though the patterns are abstract, you will find a wide black-and-red stripe, a big red-and-green plaid with white background, a very big houndstooth check, an oversize paisley more limited in use and more fatiguing to the eye than smaller-gauge menswear patterns in quieter colors and lower-contrast combinations. A tan-and-blue-gray tweed offers richness of color and pattern, but it doesn't make such an overwhelming impression that it becomes fatiguing or boring to you or to your "audience." A burgundy-and-dark-green small-scale paisley looks rich but quietly abstract. An olive-and-tan very thin stripe, or small plaid, or small geometric foulard pattern can be worn over and over again with impunity.

Finding a pattern that you like and that looks good on you is one thing. Deciding how much of it to wear, and where in an outfit to wear it, is something else. This is where many of us go wrong, especially if the pattern is a strong one in terms of size and/or color contrast.

Although I usually stick to muted tweeds and low-contrast plaids in my own wardrobe, I am occasionally attracted to very strong and definite prints. In the case that comes to mind, the print was a medium-size floral in burgundy and cream on a black background, and it came in rather dressy but simply cut silk separates. I held the print up to my face and it looked lovely, so I marched into the dressing room greedily clutching every piece the store had in my size—there must have been half a dozen of them. Fifteen minutes later I emerged with my purchase: the camisole—the smallest piece, thus the least amount of the print. What had happened? Much as I loved the print, and becoming as it was to me, I just looked overwhelmed by anything more than a small amount of it. Not only did I not look good in the camisole with the skirt or the shirt with the skirt—I didn't even look good in the shirt, or skirt, by itself. It was just too much print for me.

I find that many women are overwhelmed by too much pattern—especially a lot of the same one, and most especially if the pattern is large-scale. Be very critical about this and always try on all the pieces of a patterned outfit before you buy it. A small dose of a pattern combined with solids or other patterns may look marvelous. More of the same pattern may add up to less. You could end up looking like walking wallpaper, or as if the pattern is wearing you.

Even if the print is small-scale and in subtle colors, you have to know when to stop. Is that two-piece silk print dress in the perfect color combination really right for you? It should be: The shape is right, the colors are right, the degree of contrast is right . . . but something feels wrong. It could be too much print, or too much of that particular one. Maybe you should just buy the blouse if the pieces are sold as separates. You could wear it with the solid and tweed skirts, pants, and jackets you already own. Or you could just buy the skirt to wear out to dinner with a solid silk blouse or a lovely sweater.

I found that my print camisole worked best in summer with a black linen skirt and white linen blouse-jacket I already owned. In winter I wear it with black pants and a black sweater.

If you find it hard to determine how much of a pattern looks best on you, I would suggest that the stronger the pattern, the smaller the dose. And if you want to wear a very strong pattern in quantity, sometimes a skirt works better than a blouse—the skirt is farther away from your face, where it might seem to be in active competition with *you*.

Don't forget that there are always plenty of outfits around that couldn't look good on anyone because the pattern is so overwhelming. I assure you that even a fashion model will not look good in a pantsuit made up of a large-scale, high-contrast, white-background plaid. And no fashion model will look her best in a jacket with a skirt or a pair of pants that has very wide contrasting stripes—she'll look like a jailbird. And so will you.

Consider practicality, too. You may just love that great blanket-plaid coat, but if it's to be your one and only coat, how will it look over your entire wardrobe? (More on this in Chapter Eight.)

Although I have already gone on record about the limitations of using pattern solely with an eye toward its figure-correcting properties, there are some basic things to watch out for.

The most consistent mistake I come across is a tendency among heavier women to pick prints and plaids with a white or very light background. This can not only make you look heavier, it can also make you look unsophisticated. In most instances, a dark-background print or plaid is more slimming, more sophisticated, more citified than a light-background one. There are women who can pull off white-background plaids, but they are in the minority (a tall, slender black woman with a very dark skin and a sophisticated color sense could look striking in one). Most of us will be infinitely more flattered by a print or plaid with a dark to medium background. A floral print with a white background can make the wearer look heavy and juvenile; the same print with a black or dark background can help her look slim and sophisticated.

If you are in a store that carries large swatches of furniture fabric, step up to the nearest mirror with the plaids and prints and take a look at how you look in the same pattern with different color backgrounds. Amazing, isn't it?

Horizontal stripes across your heaviest areas are also not a good idea—especially if the stripes are wide and/or very high contrast. If they are very thin horizontal stripes, or if they are in low-contrast combinations, you may be able to get away with them.

In general, it is best to concentrate darker solids where you feel you are too heavy and prints in more neutral areas. However, if you have a small top and large bottom and you would like to wear a fullish skirt in a strong print, balance it with a solid-color loosely-fitting sweater that ends just below the waist. The bulk of the sweater will balance the print skirt—especially if you pick a sweater that is not only loose but has small shoulder pads, a dropped shoulder seam (the sleeve connects to the body of the blouse an inch or so out from where the shoulder actually ends), or a batwing sleeve.

A woman with lots of weight in her torso and very slender legs can afford to wear pants in bolder, more contrasting patterns—such as a large black-and-white houndstooth—while she sticks to a loose-fitting black sweater set on top.

If you feel you are much too thin, don't automatically rush toward an all-over look of the boldest patterns with the lightest backgrounds in the hopes of adding bulk to your look. As I mentioned before, such patterns won't look good on anyone. Consider adding more bulk to your figure with texture instead.

Another mistake many women make is in choosing what solid colors will go with a multicolor print. Many women look at such a print, see that, for example, it has red, black, blue, green, and yellow in it, and feel how lucky they are to have chosen a garment that will go with other garments or accessories in so many different colors. But such is often *not* the case. No matter how many colors in a print, there may be only one that *really* works with it—or there may be only one that is flattering enough to you to emphasize with accessories or other garments. And these may be two different colors! In the example above, black might be the only color that really works—and red might be the only color that is really becoming to you. Then you have a decision to make. And if the garment in question is not already hanging in your closet, the best decision may be to pass it by.

If you pick out every color in a print in a separate accessory, you may end up looking like a carnival queen. At the very least, you will look trendy. I won't say it can't be done—it can, if you have a really great eye—but it's very difficult, and even more difficult to make it conservatively chic.

Colors, too, can "go together" and be flattering to you, yet out of four pieces (a tan shirt, a gray shirt, a tan skirt, a gray skirt) that can be worn four different ways, some will look better than others. All possibilities are usually not equal—and the same goes for coordinating a print. So, before you decide a garment will "go with everything"—check it out in the mirror. It may go with a lot, but not with as much as you were counting on.

Combining Patterns

During the 1960s, clothing and interior designers went a little berserk and threw all sorts of patterns together. Everything went with everything else. It was very exciting for a while, but then it all got to be too much, and people retreated from it.

It *is* possible to combine patterns without looking like a shopping-bag lady. You can do it subtly and unobtrusively or dramatically and aggressively. Assuming you prefer the former, I would like to show you how to go about it, how to be absolutely certain that the results will not make you look silly.

For a foolproof pattern-combining experience, begin by sitting down and considering what two-color combination looks best on you, preferably in medium to light tones and preferably low contrast. Assume, for the sake of this example, that you pick a combination of tan and blue-gray. Then go to a store (or look through your own clothes) and pick out every small-scale menswear-pattern garment in a cut that flatters you in a tan and blue-gray combination. Try them all on together and in various combinations.

Voilà! You have perfectly coordinated pattern combinations, even if you have used six different patterns. And the effect is not wild at all. So, for the faint of heart the following rule: *You can combine any number of patterns with one another as long as you pick two colors that look good on you, those colors are medium to light shades, those colors make a low-contrast combination, you use only those two colors, and you pick only small-scale menswear patterns.*

Suppose, after a few months of this, you are heady with the success of it all and you want to branch out. Is there a logical way to proceed? I would suggest that you experiment by varying one component at a time. Sticking with the above rule, begin by varying the scale of the pattern—include one or two large-scale patterns in your mix. Or include a non-menswear pattern. Or follow the rule and use a high-contrast color combination (or a low-contrast combination of two dark tones). Use the rule but experiment with stronger colors. Or use the rule but break out of the color uniformity (include one pattern that introduces another color or colors). Do you get the idea? Don't try to vary too many factors at once until you have the feel of it.

A: *Small-scale menswear patterns in low-contrast*   *color combination.* B: *Small-scale menswear patterns in high-contrast color combination.*

A: *Menswear patterns of various scales in high-contrast color combination.* B: *Large-scale menswear and floral patterns in low-contrast color combination.* C: *Large-scale menswear and floral patterns in high-contrast color combinations — the hardest to wear.*

TEXTURE

Texture is the quietest element of chic—we tend to be more aware of its effects than of texture itself as cause.

Sometimes texture is hard to separate from pattern. A garment may have a self-pattern (say a solid-color fabric with a paisley pattern woven into it) that appears more strongly as textural variety than as pattern. Other textures are more obvious: plushy, hairy, flat, shiny, loopy, etc.

Just as a lot of women pick colors and patterns because they are "pretty" in and of themselves, so many women pick textures in the same way—without regard to how those textures look on them. A wonderful hairy tweed may be magnificent as a specimen of the weaver's art, but it may add more bulk to you than is becoming. You may just love corduroy, but if you have a full rear and the back of your corduroy skirt or pants constantly looks "sat out," i.e., bears the imprint of that full rear, corduroy is not a good choice for you, at least not in those garments.

As I suggested earlier in this chapter, textural variety is the way to make a monochromatic look interesting—the color remains constant but assorted textures vary the surfaces of the different garments. A battleship-gray wool crepe (thin, nubby wool) suit with a gray satin shirt, gray suede pumps, a gray soft glove-leather bag, and gray pearls could be very rich looking.

Texture—for example, angora, fur, thick knits—can add bulk to the very thin, or to the parts of us that appear very thin.

If you are very tall or very authoritative in your manner, you can use softer textures to soften your impact (the old iron hand in the velvet glove routine).

And texture can add a touch of femininity to a very strict business look—just change your white cotton shirt to a white silk one to see the difference.

Texture can be blatantly sexy if you use it that way: A low-cut satin dress says "touch me" in the most obvious way. But its message need not be overt, for texture can add an element of pleasant sensuality to even the most covered-up and tailored of garments. And, as I noted earlier, it affects the way a color looks on you. A very strong color will have a softer impact in a fuzzy texture (think of magenta mohair versus a magenta flat knit); a shiny texture will add light to a very dark color (black satin versus black wool crepe); and a very flat, dull texture can subdue the impact of a very wild color (orange wool crepe versus orange satin). If you love a color but feel it doesn't look that great on you—try it on in different textures. You may find one that works.

There is a lot to experiment with here. Enjoy it! Color, pattern, and texture are rich and delicious ingredients that can combine in countless beautiful ways. Even if you limit your wardrobe to your two best colors for the rest of your life, you can find thousands of ways to wear them. With an open mind and a critical eye, you can use them in the most voluptuous and flattering way—and still look conservative because of how your clothes are shaped.

For those of you who might want it as a shopping tool, the following checklist can help define potential problem areas.

SHOPPING CHECKLIST FOR COLOR, PATTERN, AND TEXTURE

Color

1. Is my hair color truly flattering to me?
2. Does my makeup foundation match my skin tone?
3. Am I wearing enough makeup for the kind of light I spend time in?
4. Are the colors I am choosing flattering to me? To my face?
5. Are the colors I am choosing appropriate for where I intend to wear them?
6. Will the colors I am choosing look right in the light I will wear them in?
7. Do my colors complement my personality?
8. Am I wearing colors that I will not be able to keep reasonably clean?
9. Are the colors I am wearing suitable for the part of the country (world) I live in? Travel to?
10. Am I taking my figure into account when I choose color?
11. Am I choosing colors just for figure "correction"? Should I?
12. Am I choosing colors just to "correct" my coloring? Should I?
13. Are my color combinations interesting or mechanical?
14. Do I always choose high-contrast color combinations? Should I?
15. If I am drawn to "classic" color combinations, have I checked that they look good on me?

Pattern

1. Am I choosing patterns that look good on me?
2. Am I choosing patterns that are appropriate for my work?
3. Am I thinking about how easily the patterns I choose will coordinate with what I already own? With new garments?

4. Do I know when a pattern is too big or too small for me?

5. Do I know how much of a pattern is too much for me?

6. Have I considered where in an outfit to wear a patterned garment?

7. Am I thinking about how quickly some patterns will bore me and others?

8. Am I taking into account how a pattern will flatter my figure?

9. Am I choosing patterns only for "corrective" purposes? Should I?

10. Am I conscious of how well the background color of my pattern works for me?

11. If combining patterns seems overwhelming to me, have I tried the rule? (Combine any small-scale menswear patterns in the same two flattering light to medium shades in a low-contrast combination.)

Texture

1. Am I picking texture that is flattering to me?

2. Am I aware of where I can wear bulkier textures without looking bulky? Or to add bulk?

3. Am I using textural variety to add interest to monochromatic looks?

4. Do I know how different textures complement my personality?

5. Am I aware that changing the texture may enable me to wear colors I didn't think I could wear?

CHAPTER FIVE

Exceptions to the Rule

Let's assume that you've put to use the information in the last two chapters and your wardrobe is now conservatively chic. The shapes of all your clothes are conservative. You've exercised taste and imagination in the colors, patterns, and textures you wear to add the element of chic. You are appropriately and attractively dressed for every occasion. And people remark about how wonderful you look.

Then one day you walk into a department store and see an outfit on a display mannequin. You try it on. It looks terrific on you, but it's very trendy. You know it will be out of style next year, but you don't care. You love it . . . you must have it . . . what to do?

Is there a way to integrate a trendy outfit into a conservatively chic wardrobe without sacrificing the look you have so carefully built up? This is an entire outfit, mind you, not just one garment.

The answer is: maybe . . . if you reverse the secret of conservative chic.

The secret of conservative chic is to wear conservatively cut garments in chic color, pattern, and texture combinations. We have already determined that it is cut or shape that makes a garment look trendy. You know that the cut of the outfit you are dying to buy is trendy and eye-catching. But you may have a choice of color or pattern combinations. Choose the quietest, most unobtrusive color/pattern combination that flatters you. Let the cut be the only eye-catcher. Consider a monochromatic look here to tone things down, or only the subtlest, most low-contrast color combination. Keep pattern minimal or low-key, too.

Don't buy such an outfit if it only comes in an orange and fuchsia lipstick print. But you might consider it in a pale-green-and-gray tweed. If it works for you in such a combination, you can sometimes wear the most way-out shapes and still appear to have some kind of continuity in your style. And you want to maintain the appearance of such continuity, because that's what gives your look a personality, a consistent quality that suggests you are a person who chooses what she wears and has a particular kind of taste, rather than an insecure person who is buffeted about by every breeze of fashion.

In Paris, I was once invited for Saturday lunch to the home of a young French woman. From this lunch, she was headed for the country, and she wore solid-color cuffed wool shorts with heavy ribbed tights, a solid-color pullover, and highly styled pumps. She was slim, had a relaxed and quiet manner, and wore a stylish (but not trendy) haircut and very little makeup. And she managed to look quietly elegant in what was actually quite a trendy outfit.

Just as you needn't buy trendy pieces to wear with other trendy pieces, you needn't wear the trendiest hairstyle, makeup, or accessories with your beloved trendy outfit. Not that any of these should be dowdy—that would look ridiculous—but they needn't be as eye-catching as the cut of your clothes.

It's okay to buy a trendy outfit now and then, just as it's okay to eat something fattening now and then. You're not a machine, and you shouldn't look like one, either. Just don't turn it into a binge that threatens your style, your wallet, or your work.

A: Trendy cut, small-scale pattern. B:Trendy cut, large-scale pattern—harder to integrate into a conservatively chic wardrobe.

CHAPTER SIX

Step Four: Accessories

Of all the dress problems women have brought to me over the years, the one that recurs with the greatest frequency is what to do about accessories. So many women complain that, though they have some idea of what is right for them when it comes to basic clothing, they have none whatsoever when it comes to accessories. And when I ask them to show me how they would accessorize one of their outfits, I see that their efforts are often mechanical, joyless, and lacking in a fundamental understanding of what accessories can do for them and for their clothing.

Some accessories, such as shoes or a handbag, have to be worn in order to make it out the door in the morning, but many (such as jewelry, belts, scarves, etc.) are worn for the pleasure and flattery they provide. Next to color, pattern, and texture, they are the most expressive element in how you dress yourself—how you present yourself to the world.

Most women are aware that accessories provide a nice finishing touch to an outfit, and they can spot another woman's talents in that regard. But when they try to put the finishing touches on their own outfits, some give up and don't accessorize at all; others retreat into boring formulas; and still others, dimly perceiving a gap of some sort, rush to fill it with just anything at all.

What is the problem here?

I think a lot of women lack experience in thinking about—and seeing—just what an accessory can and should do for them. Of course, shoes protect your feet and a handbag contains many things you will need during the day, but even for these practical accessories, there is an aesthetic dimension. And why would anyone ever bother to put on a necklace if it didn't flatter her, unless all she wanted to communicate by wearing it was her income level or status? (More about that at the end of the chapter.)

Right away, I can think of three things an accessory can do for you and your outfit:

1. *The shape of an accessory can and should harmonize with your shape and with the shapes in your outfit—likewise the color of an accessory should harmonize*

with your coloring and the colors in your outfit. You may nod in agreement because this sounds logical to you, but do you know what "harmonize" means in this context? In what ways could an accessory harmonize with your shape and the shapes in your outfit? Basically by reinforcing or echoing something about your shape or the shape of your garments, or by balancing (or sometimes "correcting") these shapes by means of contrast. And the same is true for the color of an accessory.

Let me give you some examples. Suppose you are very long from the waist down and relatively short from the waist up—mostly legs and very little midriff. You are wearing a turtleneck sweater and a pair of pants and you decide this combination needs a belt. You could tuck the sweater into the pants and wear a beautiful wide crushy suede belt; or, you could wear the sweater over the pants and wear a much narrower belt that hits you at the top of the hip rather than at your true waist. If you wear the wide belt at your true waist, it will take up precious midriff room and emphasize your short-waistedness. The lower-slung, narrower belt will drop your apparent waistline by several inches, giving you a better-proportioned look—a better balance. You must go beyond the idea that your outfit needs a belt to decide what shape belt. And worn where?

If you don't have much of a waist, but you are wearing a cream shirt-dress that looks better with a belt, you may see the same principle demonstrated with color rather than shape. A black belt might look very snappy, but the contrast will draw people's eyes to your waist. If you wear a belt in a cream or soft tan, the belt will not be as much of a focal point and your waist will be spared excessive scrutiny. You have used color to balance your shape.

If you wear a very fluid, sweeping dress and carry a hard, boxy handbag, your shapes will not be in harmony with each other. And if you wear that same dress in celadon in a soft, lightweight fabric and you stick a pair of black pumps underneath it, you might as well be wearing cement blocks on your feet—black, closed shoes will not harmonize with a dress in such a fabric and color. You would do better with a closed pump in a pale color (such as light gray), or a more open shoe or sandal in a deeper color (such as burgundy) that is not as heavy-looking as black.

Needless to say, both shape *and* color of accessories need to be in harmony with you and your outfit for optimal flattery.

2. *An accessory can add interest to your outfit.* If your wardrobe consists of simple, conservative shapes, you can construct many different looks with them, and add lots of interest to your clothes, by means of accessories.

Wear a beautiful paisley shawl in muted off-shades (taupe, burgundy, moss green, rust, navy, and blue-gray) over the shoulders of the simplest taupe pullover sweater and matching trousers; tie it under the collar of a burgundy steamer coat; drape it around a simple moss-green sweater dress; add it to a burgundy silk blouse worn with a taupe wool skirt.

Or, buy a black sweater vest with little dashes of bright color woven into it (red, white, turquoise, light green, and yellow), and wear it to add interest to an entire wardrobe of black and white. Try it over black pants worn with a plain white shirt or a plain black pullover; over a black skirt worn with a black silk shirt; over a black shirtdress; over a white shirtdress. The black will hold the bright colors in check; the bright colors add life and interest to the black.

3. *An accessory can be the focal point of your outfit.* If the accessory in question has a lot of interest on its own, and you wear it against a very simple background, it probably will be your focal point.

If you wear a dolman dress in a solid color or tiny menswear pattern and a necklace of large silver beads (say ¾-inch diameter) that just frames your face over the jewel neckline, the beads will provide a focal point. Or, if you wear that dress—or a solid-color or tiny-pattern basic blouson dress—with a large leaf pin between the neck and the shoulder, the pin will be your focal point. And such a necklace, or pin, or a simple belt with a sizeable sculptured buckle, will be the focal point of any conservatively cut, low-key combination of garments.

There is another twist on the problem of seeing what accessories can contribute to your clothes and your look. Some women choose accessories for their intrinsic beauty rather than for how they look on them. And the accessories may, indeed, be very beautiful and interesting; they may even be, in the case of jewelry, veritable objets d'art—the only trouble is, you are not a museum. You can't just hang an accessory on yourself the way you would hang a painting on the plain white wall of an empty room. No matter how beautiful the accessory in and of itself, it may not do anything beautiful for *you.*

Whenever I see a woman looking at fine gemstone jewelry against the jeweler's black velvet, I am reminded of this fact. Some women will look at a pair of emerald earrings against this backdrop and ooh and aah over the fine workmanship of the setting, the perfection of color and facet in the stones, etc. All of this may be true; unfortunately, the woman is not made out of black velvet. When she puts those earrings on, she never really sees them on herself. They may look hard and unflattering, and the color may be completely wrong for her, but she is still seeing them as objects of quality—and she may be blinded by their monetary value, as well. If she really saw herself, this woman might realize that the color of the olive-green plastic earrings she bought in the dime store is far more flattering than that of the emerald ones that blind her so.

Of course, I do not mean to put down beautiful materials and fine workmanship. Another woman might look breathtakingly beautiful in those emerald earrings. It's just that you can never look solely at the accessory, no matter what it is—you have to look at it on you. This holds true whether the accessory is earrings, a pair of shoes, a scarf, a belt, or a handbag.

When you go about the enjoyable task of choosing accessories to personalize and finish your look, try everything on and look in a mirror. And let me give you another, very important tip: Make that a full-length mirror! Often, in the departments where accessories are sold, you find only partial mirrors: mirrors that extend only a couple of feet up from the floor in the shoe department, mirrors at eye level in the scarf or the jewelry department, mirrors at waist level in the handbag department. Such mirrors are not sufficient—you should always take a look at the whole picture.

To show you why partial mirrors are insufficient, let's take a hypothetical situation. Suppose you have only a mirror on the medicine chest in your bathroom at home. When you get dressed that morning, you feel that what you are wearing could use a little something around your face. So you put on a necklace and a pair of earrings. You check it out in the bathroom mirror. It looks very nice. On the way to work, you catch sight of your reflection in a display window. The earrings with the necklace suddenly look like too much with the rest of your outfit. How could you have made such a mistake? It was simple—you just didn't see the whole picture.

A shoulder bag that hangs rather low on the hip may look all right in the waist-level department-store mirror, but when you see yourself wearing it in a full-length mirror, the bag may appear much too long for you. Perhaps you have rather short legs and that makes the bag look too close to the ground. Or it may be completely out of harmony with the kind of shoes you wear.

Or, suppose you buy a pair of shoes that look very flattering on you in the low-to-the-ground shoe-department mirror. They are so comfortable, you decide to wear them home. On the way to the elevator, you catch sight of yourself in the mirrored wall of your apartment-building lobby. What you see is a tall woman wearing shoes that are much too low for her.

Buy a full-length mirror for yourself at home and install it in a well-lit area. If you have to, travel a department away in the store and check your accessory out in the nearest full-length mirror. Get the full picture.

SHOES

Let's begin our accessories rundown with shoes, since everyone has to wear them.

The biggest problem with shoes is not looks, but comfort. I hear complaints all the time from my clients about how uncomfortable shoes are, and I'm familiar with the problem myself from the hours I spend on my feet shopping. It's not hard to understand why it is so difficult to find comfortable shoes: A shoe takes a great deal of stress, has to fit in so many places—and people's feet are unbelievably individual. Shoe sizes are general dumping grounds for everyone whose feet fall somewhere in that vicinity. If we were to confront the problem of fit and comfort honestly, we would all have our shoes custom-made . . . a pleasant idea, but one that is prohibitively expensive.

Be as alert a shoe-shopper as possible. Shoes are all cut differently, so don't just buy your size—check that the size you usually wear is right for you in this pair of shoes, and try on both halves of the pair (one foot is always a little bigger than the other, and, also, you never know what oddity may turn up in the fit or feel of the shoe you don't try on). Try on shoes after you have been on your feet for a while, and you will get a truer picture of your foot's maximum spread. Feet usually swell in summer heat, and they may also spread from wearing open sandals (don't be surprised if it is hard to wedge your feet into a pair of pumps in your winter size after a day barefoot or in sandals at the beach). You may need to buy summer shoes a half size larger.

When buying evening shoes, it's a good idea to give some thought to the effect liquor has on your feet. Most of us have a drink or two at a party or when we go out to dinner, and liquor makes many people's feet swell. You don't want those beautiful, strappy evening sandals to turn into tourniquets for the feet!

Look for real leather shoes whenever possible. Synthetics don't breathe as well and are much less comfortable.

And if you look best in high heels but feel terribly unstable on them, maybe you should consider an exercise or dance class that will build up foot, leg, and ankle strength, and help your posture (which affects how you stand on those heels) in the bargain.

Although fit and comfort are an even bigger problem than fashion, the wrong shoe can be terribly unflattering to your legs and can ruin the look of your outfit. Some shoes are ugly in and of themselves, some will look ugly on you even if they "go" with your outfit, and some will look ugly with your outfit even if they look good on your feet.

When you look at shoes, examine what they are made of and how they are put together. Disqualify shoes that are synthetic trying too hard to look like real something else. Look at how the heel joins the rest of the shoe: It should appear to grow out of the shoe, not as if the two got together by chance. Is the heel set on at an angle that looks pleasing and is flattering to your leg? A heel set too far toward the arch can be unstable and unflattering to heavy or very muscular calves; a heel set too close to the end of your heel can also be unstable and may make you look like Minnie Mouse. Look at the straps, if there are any. Are they too wide or too narrow for the rest of the shoe? Watch out for those hair-thin straps that are glued on the underside rather than stitched—when the glue loses its grip, they unfurl in the messiest possible way. And be especially aware of how any straps come out of the body of the shoe—there should be no awkwardness in the transition.

As with anything else you wear, be certain that any ornamentation really adds to the look of the shoe and that it won't limit coordination possibilities. Go for as little extraneous detail as possible unless you already have lots of basics.

Heel height and shape is important to consider. Don't be a tall person who automatically reaches for the lowest heels going—extremely low heels on a very tall woman will make her look gawky. If you're tall, you're tall; make the most of it. You can wear even very high heels without looking silly. By the same token, don't be a short woman who always reaches for the highest heels—very high heels on a short woman look juvenile, too, as if she were playing dress-up in her mother's clothes.

Watch out for very narrow heels if you have heavy or very muscular calves— a bit of width in your heel, even in high evening shoes, will help balance your calf. T-straps are unflattering to a wide calf, too—for some reason the calf looms larger than life above that skinny vertical—and to very narrow feet, because they call attention to that narrowness.

Some fashion texts will tell you that ankle straps are unflattering, especially if your legs are not the slimmest. While that is probably true if your ankles are wide and unshaped, I wouldn't consider it a rule—it depends on a lot of different relativities in the leg-ankle-foot area and on just where the ankle strap hits you and how it fastens. I wouldn't say you need to be any more critical about ankle straps than about any other kind of shoe straps.

Conservative Shoe Shapes

The pump. This is the most basic and versatile shoe shape in your wardrobe, and there is a variation of it to flatter every woman. Heavier pumps with low, broad, sometimes stacked (built up of horizontal layers of leather) heels can be very sporty, make good walking shoes, and look very nice with pants. Delicate, low-cut pumps with high, slender heels can be very dressy. And there are lots of possibilities in between. The simpler they are, the greater the versatility of your pumps.

If your budget is so limited that you can afford only one pair of good-quality shoes, they should probably be cordovan to burgundy in color with medium-height heels.

A conservative pump could also have an open toe or a strap across the instep.

The spectator. The classic spectator is a two-tone pump with perforated heel and toe detail—and the classic combinations are a white shoe with black, luggage, or navy heel and toe. In those seasons when spectators receive renewed attention from shoe designers, you can often find other, more exotic color combinations (such as a medium-brown shoe with dull-green toe and heel). If the shoe is still conservatively shaped, and the color combination is unusual but works well with the colors you wear, this is still a conservative choice, and often a very chic one.

You will sometimes find a solid-color shoe referred to as a spectator if it sports the classic spectator perforated detail. Such a shoe is often an excellent choice for pants.

Spectators can go a long way toward making a conservative business outfit look chic without any sacrifice of businesslike feeling. Luggage and white is the most basic combination—but if your wardrobe is basically black or navy, you may be better served by one of those colors.

The sling-back. The basic sling-back has a closed toe and a medium-to-high heel, although sling-backs can be found with open toes as well. Check carefully that you have the right length in these shoes—you don't want your heel to flop over the edge of the shoe, and you don't want extra shoe protruding past the end of your heel, either. And the same goes for an open toe—your toes should neither flop over the end nor lie too far back from it, leaving an oddly empty space.

If you buy solid-color sling-backs, bone, tan, or gray is a versatile choice. The classic sling-back is the Chanel style, a sort of spectator of sling-backs: It is a bone shoe with a black toe piece (and, sometimes, a black heel). Such a shoe should always be worn with a stocking toned to the bone.

The sling-back is a good example of what I was cautioning you about on the transition from shoe to strap. Look carefully at the point where shoe becomes sling to ascertain if that is gracefully accomplished—the strap should appear to grow out of the body of the shoe rather than bridge the shortest distance between two points.

The T-strap. If you have slender calves and ankles, the T-strap can help vary your shoe wardrobe. As I've already indicated, it is not a good choice for women with wider ankles or calves, or with extremely narrow feet. It can look nice with a suit or a tailored dress, but, because the T part of the strap is a very strong detail, check to see if it isn't too busy-looking with the other details in your outfit. If you love T-straps and they are not becoming to your legs, wear them in a shade as close to your skin tone as possible to minimize their unflattering effect.

The sandal. Heeled sandals come in many different varieties. If you work, you need to determine not only shape and color, but also whether or not sandals are really appropriate. Some offices are so conservative that women who work there feel out of sync in a shoe with any openness whatsoever. In others, an open-toe sling-back or pump seems okay as long as the opening is minimal, and, in still others, just about anything goes that does not look outright beachy.

Never wear sandals without a careful check of how well-groomed your toes are. They should be neatly manicured, the nails carefully trimmed and polished. I'm always amazed at how many women wear sandals to work with uneven, grimy, unpolished toenails. Nothing looks worse! And if you work in a conservative office, pick something other than flaming fuchsia for the color of your toenail polish. Unpolished toenails in open-toe shoes look underdressed.

For maximum flattery check heel height and width, gracefulness of straps, and heel and toe fit on your sandals. A medium tan is a good all-purpose color choice, and black is good if you wear a lot of black—with the added benefit that you can wear a black sandal with certain colors with which you could not wear a black pump (the pump would look too heavy).

The moccasin. This is a very broad category of shoe that covers just about everything in the loafer-fringe-tassel area. Always on the sporty side, moccasins run the gamut from low-heeled loafers (plain, fringed, or tasseled), to an elegant and dainty, higher-heeled shoe with a narrow little fringe at the front, to wear with a suit. A medium-height moccasin with a broad stacked heel makes a great pants shoe. Avoid metal details (horseshoes, bits, etc.) and stick to the self-details (such as fringes and tassels).

Because moccasins come in such a wide variety of styles, there is at least one

SHOES AND BOOTS

A.

B.

C.

Column A: *Pump; Open-toe pump; Strap pump; Spectator; Solid-color spectator.* Column B: *Sling-back; Chanel-style sling-back; T-strap; Sandal, sling-back; Sandal, ankle-strap.* Column C: *Dressy moccasin; Sporty moccasin; Pull-on boot.*

for every woman. The classic—and very versatile—colors for moccasins are cordovan or luggage.

Shoe Color

I have already made some remarks about shoe color, so part of this will be recapitulation, but I think it helps to have this kind of information in one place.

Black shoes do not go with everything, despite what your mother may have told you. As a matter of fact, black pumps don't go with very much—unless you wear a lot of black. They can add a weighty and frumpy touch to colored garments, as in the example on page 88. Black sandals are more versatile (the straps make the black look airier). If you do wear a lot of black, black shoes of all varieties are your best choice. For a more sophisticated look and one that can add length to your legs, try your black shoes with sheer black or dark gray stockings. While this may be too much for the extremely conservative office, you will not look way-out in most instances if you dress conservatively.

Navy shoes also do not go with everything. The color area that does go with everything is cordovan to burgundy. And the next most versatile color area is tan to bone.

If shoes provide the interest or focal point to an outfit, they can be one very bright color, or multicolor. And sometimes you get a very interesting look if the shoes don't really match anything in the outfit—they can provide just the color accent that brings out everything else (but it takes a sophisticated color sense to do this right).

Should shoes match bag and/or belt? A qualified yes . . . that is, yes, unless you are very good with color. They needn't match in texture, though.

BOOTS

There is not much to worry about if you want conservatively chic boots. What you are looking for is a pair of medium-heel boots that pull on (no zipper) and end just below the knee. Cordovan is the color that will work with just about anything. They should have no ornamentation whatsoever. The problem is in the fit—women with large calves as well as those with very high insteps may have a hard time finding a pull-on pair with enough room to allow for these problems. However, a zipperless boot is infinitely preferable to a zippered one in terms of simplicity and beauty of line, for a zipper adds no more to the look of your boot than it does to the look of the back of your dress. If you must buy a zippered pair, try to find one where the zipper is as unobtrusive as possible.

Don't wear boots at work (to and from is another matter) if you work in a very conservative field, or if the suits and dresses you wear are consistently on the formal side. Boots can be casually elegant—but they are casual. Unmatched separates, sweater separates, and longish full skirts all look particularly good with boots; if that is how you dress for work, you should be able to wear them at work, too. Otherwise, save your beautiful boots for weekends and your own time, where they can give a more relaxed look to some of your working wardrobe as well as to sportier clothing.

Rain or snow boots. It can be quite a challenge to find a decent-looking pair of these, especially for work. Again, cordovan to burgundy, black (if you wear that color a lot), or brown is your best bet. They should be the same height and style as your leather boots, and as simple as possible.

HANDBAGS, BRIEFCASES, CARRYALLS

These are all accessories where the first criterion is convenience. What works for one woman in size and shape may not work for another. The most beautiful handbag is a flop if you can't find anything in it. This is an area you should give a lot of thought to—go through your needs, habits, and preferences very carefully.

Convenience is one reason for careful thought here, but another reason is need; that is, you shouldn't need a great many of these accessories, and you probably don't have the time to change them, either.

Certainly, if you work, you are going to buy one good briefcase, rather than several. So you need to know what you will be carrying in it to decide about size and compartments.

One really nice carryall is also better than a lot of not-so-terrific ones. Think about what you usually carry around with you in extras and choose the size and shape accordingly.

And, even in the handbag area, I think it is better to have one very good one that goes with everything and has the size and interior you are comfortable with than to have a lot of possibilities, even if they are beautiful. After all, who has time today for changing from one handbag to another?

Handbags

If you are, or want to be, a one-basic-handbag lady, you need to be very certain about what you are looking for. How large a bag do you need to carry your necessaries? What is the most basic accessory color for your particular ward-

CLUTCH BAGS

A.

B.

C.

SHOULDER BAGS

Column A: *Envelope clutch; Two styles of frame clutch; Half-melon clutch.* Column B: *Hobo; Duffel; Stiff straw pouch; Chanel-style shoulder bag.* Column C: *Satchel; Curved envelope shoulder bag; Camera-case shoulder bag.*

BRIEFCASES

CARRYALLS

robe? If you tend toward a larger bag, is it so large that you are dwarfed by it? Or, if you are a big or tall woman who loves tiny bags, how do they look on you? How hard are you on a bag—if you knock it around a lot, would you be better off picking a textured rather than a smooth surface, or a fabric that can take abuse? What style bag will coordinate effectively with the kind of clothes you wear—and cover a certain range of possibilities?

If you can answer all these questions for yourself, you may find that you have designed your ideal bag with the answers. Now all you have to do is find it!

I divide the handbag world into two areas: clutches and shoulder bags. You have to decide which is most convenient for you, but I can point out some of the salient qualities of each type.

Many women find shoulder bags most convenient, for they leave the hands free. If you have to carry a lot of things, including, possibly, a small child, a shoulder bag definitely offers advantages. But, because you needn't hold on to it, it can make you very vulnerable to purse-snatchers and pickpockets.

If you wear a fur, a shoulder bag is not a good choice, for the strap will cause wear along the shoulder of your coat or jacket. And, if you often have to carry a tote to accommodate things too large to fit into your handbag, you are probably better off with a clutch, which you can slip into the tote or carryall more neatly than a shoulder bag.

If you choose a shoulder bag, think about size, shape, color, texture, how long the strap should be (a very long strap will look odd on a short woman; a very short strap will look odd on a tall woman), and whether or not the bag hits you at an unflattering point because of the strap length. The shape, as well as the color and material, can make a shoulder bag look more or less dressy. A very large shoulder bag is always sporty; a small-to-medium-size one can be dressier. For a dressier look choose a simple pouch, camera case, envelope or curved envelope, or quilted Chanel style. A drawstring, duffel, hobo, or half-melon style will be sportier.

A clutch bag is usually a bit more versatile than a shoulder bag. If you choose a very simple one in a nice leather, suede, or snake, it can go from sporty to quite dressy occasions. But, as the name indicates, you must clutch it to hold onto it. If you are the kind of person who can't stand holding things and frequently put your bag down and walk away from it, you may not have it long. You might be better off with a shoulder bag.

As I said, you can very easily slip a clutch into a carryall. And, if you are trying to keep your lines as simple as possible, having no shoulder strap means having one less line to busy up your outfit. Classic clutches come with framed tops or as various kinds of envelopes.

Once you already have your basic bag, you can turn your attention to two additional possibilities: a somewhat dressy bag (if your basic is a shoulder bag, this might be a clutch) and an out-and-out evening bag. Of course, both of these should be basics for the kinds of clothes you will be wearing them with.

As with shoes, keep trim minimal here. For one thing, it limits a bag's versatility; for another, metal trim almost inevitably tarnishes, which is a pain in the neck.

Briefcases

I divide briefcases into two types, also: hard-sided and soft-sided. And I have yet to see the woman who didn't look better carrying a soft-sided one (or the man, either, for that matter). They are simply more graceful and less clunky.

For the most conservatively chic look, carry a leather envelope with absolutely no hardware on it. Unless you wear almost nothing but black, you will be best off with cordovan, burgundy, tan, or luggage. If you need a briefcase with handles, choose a soft-sided one with no extraneous trim.

Much has been written about what to, and what not to, carry in your briefcase. I feel it's up to you to figure out how to handle this. So long as the effect is businesslike, it doesn't really matter—if you keep makeup in yours, just don't display it.

Carryalls

Here again, simplicity is all. Give the cutesy ones to your kids. Never buy a carryall with something written or pictured on it. A plain leather or canvas shopping bag in a solid color—your neutral accessories color, or something that works with both your clothes and your accessories—with no trim is ideal. Beware of multicolor ones—what will they go with? A carryall is perceived as part of what you are wearing, just as a handbag is. Use the same criteria in selecting it!

BELTS

The first consideration with a belt is whether you want to wear one at all. Belts call attention to your waistline, and if you don't have much of a waist, or if you carry a lot of your weight there, you may not want to wear one. Perhaps you would look better in an unbroken tunic line, or an unbelted sweater worn over (rather than tucked into) the waistband of your skirt or pants. If you do want to wear a belt, wear a jacket, vest, or sweater open over your outfit (that way one doesn't see enough of your waistline for the belt to do any damage). Or, tone your belt so closely to what you are wearing it over that it doesn't stand out.

The basic conservatively chic belt is a fairly narrow (about ⅝ inch) leather belt with a covered buckle (no hardware to tarnish or compete with jewelry). Next most basic is the same style belt in a slightly wider width (about ⅞ inch). When in doubt always choose a covered buckle—it is much more versatile than a hardware one, and it has a look of quiet elegance that is one of the hallmarks of conservative chic.

If you do buy a belt with a metal buckle, think of that buckle as jewelry. Will it compete with the jewelry you wear around your face or on your wrists and hands? If you wear mostly gold or gold-plated jewelry, a simple brass buckle can be nice. And, if you tend toward silver, a belt with a silver or silvery buckle is okay. But the design of the buckle should be up to jewelry standards—the shape and all details should be really pleasing and flattering to you, whether you are purchasing a brass bridle-bit buckle, a sculptured silver one, or an imitation silver cowboy belt.

Another way to get around dealing with an aggressive belt buckle (other than buying a belt with a covered buckle) is to buy a sash, which has no buckle at all. A sash can be a simple leather or fabric tape, or a leather or fabric narrow tube (these usually look best if you knot the ends). It could also be, for variety's sake, a square or rectangular scarf that you have folded lengthwise and then twisted into a tubular shape and tied in a bow or knot—or (à la Fred Astaire) a man's tie that you have knotted to one side of your waist. Picture this last in a quiet burgundy foulard (small geometric) print knotted around the waist of your navy suit skirt and worn with a navy silk blouse and matching jacket. Everything in this outfit is very subdued, but the fact that the belt is a man's tie adds just the smallest touch of whimsy.

A cummerbund also gets around the buckle problem, although it is a rather specific style that doesn't work with everything. Better than the old-fashioned pleated kind is a long, wide, leather or fabric tape that you can wrap and twist around your waist in a number of different ways. A cummerbund really calls attention to your waist, so before you buy one, be sure it can stand the scrutiny. You needn't wrap it so tightly that you can't breathe, but it does look best on a small waist. And it is a strong and eye-catching accessory, so you can't have too many other big accessory statements with it.

What about the belt as jewelry? If a belt is made out of real gold, silver, or some other precious or semi-precious material, the style is flattering to you, you have a waist that can stand lots of attention, and you minimize your other

A.

BELTS

B.

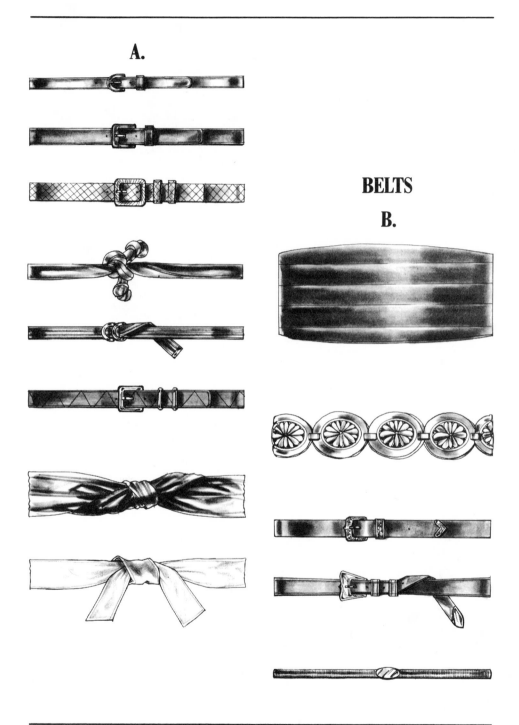

Column A: *Two narrow covered-buckle belts; Woven belt; Tubular sash; Double-ring tape;*
Stitched belt; Two sashes. Column B: *Cummerbund; Navajo belt; Cowboy belt; Variation on a*
cowboy belt; Narrow expansion belt.

jewelry, fine—especially if you wear very simple clothing. But I am not a big fan of fake silver or gold chains or expandable metal belts. They often look cheap and garish on a garment in a fine fabric, or in conjunction with real jewelry.

If a belt at your waist is not becoming, you can always consider a simple and more loosely fitted hip-riding style, especially on top of an overblouse or a sweater worn over a waistband. If your problem is not one of real weight in the center of your body but simply an undefined waist, this can be a very successful solution.

SCARVES AND SHAWLS

Knowing what to do with a scarf can make the difference in even the simplest and least expensive wardrobe. And, if you learn what is right for you in this area, you can accomplish a great deal in the style department with even one or two well-chosen ones.

Many women think of a scarf inevitably as a printed silk square or rectangle. It needn't be. A solid-color (one that looks good near your face) scarf in a beautiful fabric could be the most versatile item in your entire wardrobe. Like a blouse in such a color, try it with clothes you don't feel it "goes" with, and let yourself be surprised by what it can do for the look of your outfit.

A short menswear-pattern muffler in muted tones that are flattering to you is another wonderful scarf to have in silk or wool. Some very small-scale or low-contrast menswear patterns are almost as versatile as solids. Try these, too, with things they don't seem to go with.

When I teach my clients how to wear scarves, I usually begin by telling them that a scarf should have a sort of just-happened, not-too-tidy look about it . . . as if you threw it at your outfit, and that was the way it landed. Carefully tied and perfectly symmetrical bows and knots are much less interesting to look at than asymmetrical off-center looks—especially if the rest of what you are wearing is all lined up with the buttons of your blouse.

And you needn't learn a hundred and three ways to tie a scarf to get mileage out of it, either. All you need is one or two flattering ways that you really know how to manage.

Not every woman looks good in the same scarf size or shape. I find the small squares and the skinny rectangles (whether long or short) the most versatile. And I often twist both of these so that they don't take up too much room on the neck.

SHAWLS

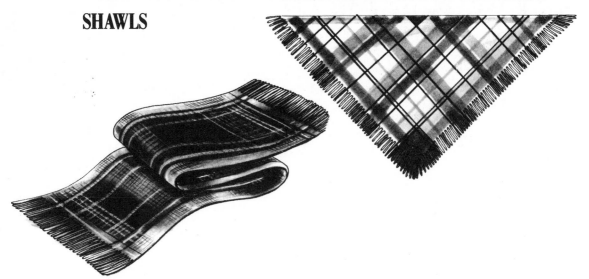

If I were to name my favorite of all the many ways to tie a scarf, it would be the one-loop bow. To do this, take a small square and fold it once into a triangle; take the shortest point and fold it in to the midpoint between the two long points, then overlap in the same direction until you have a long, narrow shape; twist the scarf, holding onto both ends, until it looks like a thick necklace; wrap the scarf around your neck and tie it in a bow, but pull the second loop completely through, so that the bow has only one loop and two ends; move the loop off-center on your neck. You can do the same thing with a short or long skinny rectangle. You won't have to fold it; you only have to twist it. And, if it is a very long scarf, wrap it one or more times around your neck before tying in front in the one-loop bow. You may want to tuck the ends into the neck of your blouse or jacket for a neater look.

Of course, there are hundreds of other ways to tie a scarf. And, of those hundreds, there are surely any number that would look good on you. No matter how conservatively you dress, you should always be open to new ideas about how to tie scarves. Look at the better fashion magazines (such as *Vogue*), at store window displays, and at women who wear scarves well. Consider wearing a scarf with your more basic coats, suits, sweater dresses, dresses, and separates. Wear a scarf instead of jewelry for a change. Try unexpected (but flattering) colors and prints; a scarf as a belt; two scarves worn together.

I find the larger square scarves more difficult to deal with—they take up too much room around the neck and shoulders. The small squares and narrower (or folded) rectangles are easier to fit under a collar, inside a neckline, or around your waist. A skinny rectangle of a fabric tie can also be a nice item to fool around with. Try knotting the ends before you tie it. And don't wear it like a bogus man's tie with a tailored shirt and a business suit—that looks like you're trying too hard . . . or joking.

Aside from length and shape, consider the weight of any scarf you buy. If you plan to wear it around your neck, make sure that your choice is not too bulky for the length of your neck—or the size of your bosom. And the scarf should also not be too heavy for the outfit you are wearing it with.

If you love jewel-neck pullovers but feel that your neck is not what it once was, learn how to tie scarves artistically. The simplicity of the jewel-neck pullover is the perfect background for an interesting scarf collection.

Because you usually wear a scarf near your face, never buy one in a color or print that is not very becoming to your face—no matter how well it "goes" with your outfit.

Shawls

A shawl is a wonderful and versatile item to own. Here again, a simple one in a very becoming solid color can do a lot for your wardrobe. Buy a large, rather than a skimpy, size, so that you can really wrap it around you. Use it as an evening wrap over a bare dress. Tie it around the shoulders of your steamer coat to add warmth and color or pattern. Wear it over a suit for those days with a chill in the air when you aren't yet ready for a coat. Drape it over a long-sleeve wool dress, a sweater and pants, or a blouse and skirt, for warmth and a little bit of drama. A lightweight wool or cashmere shawl in an interesting, muted, off-shade—such as a gray lavender—could work in any of these situations and with an enormous variety of colors, looking dressy or casual, while a "dressy" evening shawl—say, black with a gold thread design—will go with very little.

If you have a large or protruding rear, you may be better off with a rectangular rather than a square shawl; the square shawl gets folded into a triangle, and the point of that triangle is like an arrow leading right to your seat. Avoid long, drippy fringe unless your clothes are very simple and undetailed.

Because a shawl is a luxurious, snuggly item to cuddle into, pick a beautiful soft fabric when you buy one, such as mohair, cashmere, silk, or a fine, soft wool. Steer clear of harsh-looking synthetics if you can afford to.

JEWELRY AND WATCHES

Your two most basic jewelry decisions are: what style of jewelry looks best on you (for instance, strong, weighty, and sizeable versus tiny, dainty, and filigree) and where on your body you should place it.

When I was a teenager, my school offered a jewelry-making minicourse in our regular art class. All the pieces I turned out for myself were dainty little filigree numbers of twisted wire. "That's funny," the art teacher, a rather brusque woman, said as she ambled past the table where I was working. "That's not at all the way I see you. Those pieces are too dainty for you—you have a stronger look than that!"

I hated the art teacher passionately from that day onward. She had made me feel like a clunk, when I wanted to think of myself as sweetly and delicately feminine. But today I know she was right, and I don't feel any less feminine for it: I look my best in stronger, weightier pieces of jewelry or in something very exotic—tiny gold posies are not my style.

Try to steer clear of clichés when you determine your own jewelry style. Sometimes a small woman looks good in rather large pieces of jewelry. If you like to wear jewelry around your face and you have a fairly large head for your size and/or strong or sizeable facial features, the chances are you will look better in a stronger jewelry look, even if you are short. And if you are large-boned, you probably will, too, regardless of your height.

A woman with a small head and/or small facial features may look lovely in dainty little pieces of jewelry around her face. And a woman with a rather plain but not strong-featured face may be transformed by them.

Strong jewelry is not better than dainty jewelry or vice-versa. What is important is what works on you. No matter how pretty, strong, dainty, or artistic the jewelry is on its own, when you wear it, it is in the service of your looks.

Once you have an idea of what type of jewelry flatters you, you have to decide on the optimal position for it in your own geography.

I should admit to a personal bias here: I feel that most women are more flattered by jewelry around their faces than around their wrists and fingers. Jewelry worn near the face is yet another way to surround it with flattering color and, in the case of shiny metal jewelry, with additional light as well. But this should not sway you if you have good reasons for feeling otherwise.

Then, too, some women seem to look their best in lots of jewelry, and others need only the minimum, such as a tiny pair of diamond stud earrings.

When you decide where to put your jewelry, take a moment to think about how that affects your other possible jewelry locations. You can't load up fingers, wrists, neck, and ears without looking like a gypsy (gypsies are not conservatively chic). A lot of jewelry in one area will probably mean less in others.

Beware of matched sets. Like matching bedroom sets, there is usually at least one piece that is too much. As I already mentioned in the chapter on color, too matching is often too much. It can look unimaginative and insecure. If you have sets of jewelry, and if the pieces are too much together, simply mix some of those pieces with other jewelry or wear them singly.

Earrings

Earrings are my choice for the most important jewelry item. They are not only near your face, they are actually on your face, so they can do a lot to reflect light and flattering color on the part of you that most people look at, and they also give a more "dressed" look to whatever you are wearing.

There are five different kinds of earrings: studs, earrings that rest on the lobe, hoops, small drops, and dangles. Studs are the most basic if you have pierced ears, and you can find tiny to quite sizeable ones in gold, diamond, pearls, and other precious stones, semi-precious stones (such as jade), and costume jewelry. A small pair of diamond studs is a rather basic investment for many women (and the tiny ones are often more flattering, less rocklike, than the big ones)—they can be worn with just about anything.

Many women look better and more dressed in earrings larger than studs that fill the earlobe in either pierced, screw-on, or clip-on styles. Because these are larger, they offer a more flattering dose of color and light than a tiny stud would. If you work, and/or you don't want to get tired of your earrings quickly, choose geometric shapes (circles, squares, rectangles, triangles, ovals, twists, etc.) or such quiet representational shapes as shells, leaves, or fans. Leave the flowers and smiling cats to others.

Hoop earrings are a classic, and they are certainly okay in most situations, but they have become something of a cliché. They look a little too preppy nowadays. If you have them, wear them with a peasant blouse to a bistro on the weekend.

That brings us to small drops, which occasionally look all right in a business situation—a small silver teardrop can be nice. But once you move off the ear (and this goes for hoops, too), you are entering dangerous waters for business, and you also should check to see that such styles are not too busy-looking for the rest of your outfit.

Large dangles are costumey, aren't appropriate for work, and are unflattering if you have a short neck. They are also very dressy, and rarely look good with the rather tailored sportswear most of us wear most of the time.

Do not be a precious jewelry snob unless you have good reason to think that nothing else is becoming to you. As a matter of fact, more women look better in the rich, warm off-shades of many semi-precious stones than in the colder, truer, more glittering colors of precious ones. You may be an exception here, but it's something to think about. And there are plenty of costume jewelry earrings that don't pretend to be gold and silver in attractive shapes and colors, too.

Don't automatically choose gold rather than silver because it is more valuable. Many women look better in silver.

Necklaces

Because they sit right under your face, necklaces can be another enormous source of flattery. Length is crucial. Basic necklace lengths are: choker (wrapped around the neck), collar (resting on the collarbone), between collar and breast, and those that fall onto or over the breast.

With necklaces, particularly, check the effect in a full-length mirror, for what looks lovely around the face may be completely out of sync with the rest of your outfit and proportions. I think the collar length suits many women—and it's brief enough not to interfere with other clothing details. If this length is becoming to you, consider a collar-length string of pearls or semi-precious stones (coral, turquoise), a simple gold chain, large silver beads, ivory beads, wooden beads, and a very plain rigid or jointed gold or silver collar.

If you look better in the traditional necklace length (between collarbone and breast), you can consider all of the above as well as lariats, lockets, and pendants (avoid cutesy hearts-and-flowers with the latter two). If this is not the best length for you, but you have a nice strand of pearls that you do not wish to shorten, wear it inside an open shirt collar, where you get just a glimpse of it now and then.

Very long necklaces (what used to be called opera length in pearls) are something I feel you should approach with caution. I know that magazine articles tout them as a strong vertical that works well with a full bustline, but I'm not so sure that's always true. Long beads can sit on a full bustline (or fall off the end of it) as if on a shelf. Maybe necklaces just aren't your best bet if you are that busty.

If you're not terribly busty, a long pendant on a cord or chain might look nice, but I don't think I would wear one to a conservative office—such necklaces dangle low enough to flop around as you walk, or make noise as they swing against furniture, which can be rather distracting.

If you decide to buy Oriental or cultured pearls, be aware that they come in quite a variety of whites—you can find fine pearls with a gray, pink, or yellow cast to them. Choose the shade that flatters your skin tone, not the one that seems "prettiest" to you.

Pins

If your shoulders are so small that a necklace often seems to take up too much space, consider wearing two or even three pins slightly to one side of the neckline of what you are wearing. You'll get something of the effect of a necklace without the bulk—and you'll have an interesting off-center detail. In the thirties and forties, there were lots of costume jewelry clip pins in abstract shapes (and, often, in interesting colors) that are perfect for adding interest to a jewel-neck sweater or blouse. You can still find them in thrift and inexpensive antiques shops.

Pins come in geometric and representational shapes. If you wear a representational pin to work, consider a leaf shape rather than a dog; however, a cameo is usually abstract enough not to cause a problem. Geometric shapes are fine for work—just avoid the aggressive and hard-edged bad designs that look like some "decorative" piece you might find on the coffee table of a bachelor pad.

There is nothing wrong with wearing several pins together, if the whole is more than the sum of its parts. And, if pins look good on you, here is an area to build an interesting and personal collection. A couple of stickpins worn side by side can be a very delicate jewelry accent.

A pin worn smack in the center of a neckline has an old-fashioned, retrospective look. This can be charming, demure, and innocent with an antique-looking lace or linen blouse, but it can also be both boring and aging with a more contemporary look. So much of the clothing and accessories we wear is symmetrical; a pin is one of the more obvious ways to break up that symmetry a bit. If you wear your pins front and center, just be sure you're getting the effect you want.

Bracelets

I am not a big fan of bracelets, partly because I am not very comfortable in them myself. For me, they get in the way of things and often contribute more clutter than flattery. However, you may feel otherwise, or you may like to wear bracelets in certain situations.

If you wear a tailored watch, and you want to soften the look of it with a bracelet, a simple bangle or flat chain in a metal that matches that of the watch is most becoming. And a simple flat chain bracelet looks nice without a watch.

Bangles (bracelets of rigid material that fit the arm somewhat above the wrist) can come in the most wonderful sculptured oval or circular shapes, but they can also make an awful clatter if they slip down to the wrist. Needless to say, this is not for work.

JEWELRY AND WATCHES

A.

B.

C.

D.

E.

F.

G.

A: *Studs.* B: *Earrings that rest on the lobe.* C: *Hoops.* D: *Drop; Dangle.* E: *Choker and choker necklaces.* F: *Traditional-length necklaces.* G: *Long pendant; long necklace.*

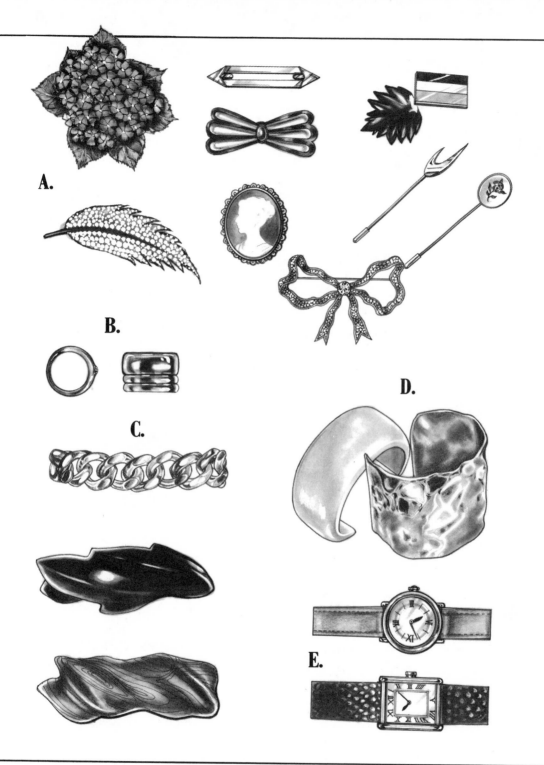

A. *Bunch of violets; Pins; Clip pins; Stick pins.* **B.** *Rings.* **C.** *Flat chain bracelet; Bangles.* **D.** *Cuffs.* **E.** *Watches.*

One of the most elegant, versatile, and quiet bracelets is a fitted cuff. These are not for the heavy-armed, but they look very nice on a wide variety of women, and they can work with a variety of clothes, from a sweater to a cocktail dress. However, the really broad ones can be constricting to the muscles in your forearm.

Rings

If you wear a very eye-catching ring, it will call attention to your hands. If you have pretty hands, this may be no problem. But if your hands are not one of your best features, and/or they are in somewhat ragged shape, don't subject them to such scrutiny. Wear a simple band or two, or forget about rings entirely.

The most common mistake I see women make with rings is to choose a style that is much too dressy for the kind of clothes they ordinarily wear. Again, it's that old out-of-context bugaboo. A woman may love a ring in and of itself—and she makes no effort to consider it in the context of her looks and life-style. There are plenty of beautiful rings out there that are not the digital equivalent of a tiara. Put your money into a ring you can wear with everything, or almost everything, unless you can afford lots of them.

A ring on every finger is better in a nursery rhyme. Such a look is distracting at work, and even in a lot of social situations. There is also a slight creepiness to it, as if you had deliberately immobilized your hands.

Rings should be chosen to fit your life-style, wardrobe, fingers, and skin tone. Don't buy a ring with a stone in an unflattering color no matter how gorgeous it looks.

Watches

If you wear a watch, choose one that has some relation to your bone structure and the kind of clothes you wear. A big, clunky sports watch does not look right with a business suit or on a really tiny wrist. Pick a watch with a large enough face so that you can see it without squinting, but choose a simple circle or rectangle that won't draw attention away from the rest of what you are wearing. The strap should be leather or some other skin in a color that coordinates with your wardrobe—or in a metal that coordinates but does not compete with your jewelry.

Don't buy a watch that is too big or too small for you, and don't buy the watch of the moment—buy something you are comfortable in that looks tasteful and serious but doesn't cry status. Items of dress that cry status also bespeak insecurity, especially if you wear more than one at a time.

HATS AND GLOVES

Gloves

Although gloves are not the fashion accessory they were in the days when women wore them for a well-dressed look rather than solely for warmth, they can still add a nice accent to a coat or suit.

I find that many women either buy gloves that they think are basic but that add nothing in looks, or they pick gloves that are "pretty" but bear no relation to the outfit they'll wear them with. You can avoid both of these extremes when you go shopping by remembering what you intend to wear your gloves with and then choosing a color that complements or adds an element of tasteful surprise to your coat.

Forget about trimming and fancy details and concentrate on color. And, since gloves (unless they are leather) are not terribly expensive, buy more than one pair to change the look of your basic solid-color or tweed coat. But remember the colors of your other accessories (shoes, boots, bag, mufflers, etc.) when making your selection.

Because gloves are not worn near your face, you can even pick a color that is interesting but not so flattering. Think of bright-red gloves with a dark brown coat and stacked-heel moccasins—or even a dash of chartreuse. Try olive green—or blue-violet—with a camel coat and luggage pumps.

Basic gloves come in two-button (just covering the wrist) and four-button (extending to mid-forearm) lengths. Wool or leather is your best choice. Synthetics are not that warm. Leather gloves need to be cleaned (expensively) from time to time, depending on how light they are in color and how much dirt you come in contact with. It is better to own two pairs of nice wool gloves that you can wash yourself or clean cheaply than one beautiful pair of leather ones that you cannot afford to keep up.

Hats

Hats also used to be a hallmark of a well-dressed lady, whether she needed to keep her head warm or not. If you live in a warm climate or you don't mind the cold, you might never find a reason to wear one these days; but if you do decide to wear one for looks or warmth, choose carefully. I have seen a lot of women who looked perfectly dressed from the earlobes down ruin the whole thing with the wrong hat.

Unless you really know what you are doing, avoid any hat with a deep crown. Some women resort to these because they feel such a hat will give them

HATS AND GLOVES

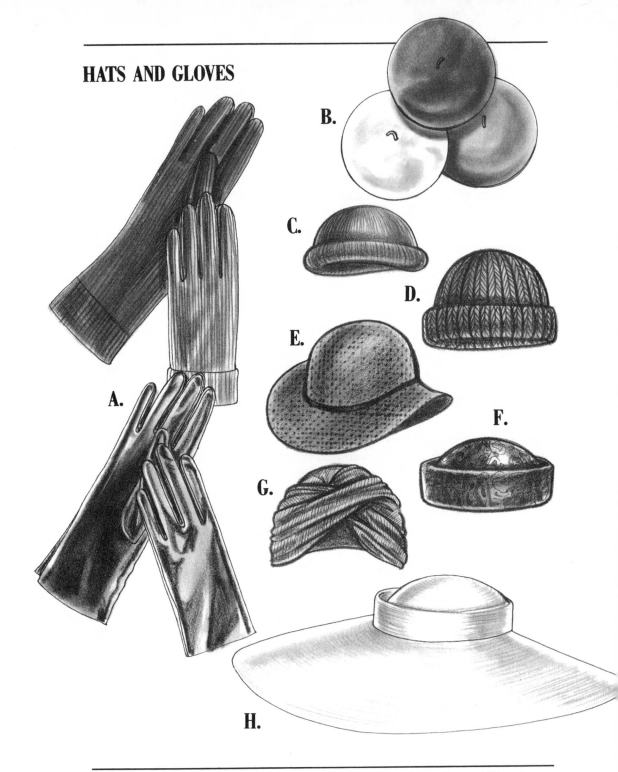

A: *Gloves.* B: *Berets.* C: *Dressy watch cap.* D: *Watch cap.* E: *Small-brim hat.* F: *Pillbox.* G: *Turban.* H: *Picture hat.*

"height," but it can actually make them look foreshortened, in the same way a too-long jacket can. And even if it does give them "height" it looks matronly and unstylish. The hats that have been mainstream for the last I-don't-know-how-many years have all had flat crowns: berets, small-brim hats, knitted watch caps, turbans, etc. If some version of these does not flatter you, perhaps it is better to forgo a hat for most occasions. But, before you decide that a beret or a small-brim hat is unflattering, try tilting it a bit. There is an art to knowing how to wear a hat, and how to use it to frame your face effectively.

Other hats fall into the category of classic costume hats. A straw sailor, a large-brim (flat-crown) picture hat, or a tiny black pillbox with a veil might conceivably act as accents to certain conservative chic looks on an occasional or special-occasional basis. These never go out of style if they are becoming to you, but they are too costumey for work or for the average person's social life.

A classic costume hat might be ornamented, because it is a once-in-a-while item anyway. If it is, be certain that the ornamentation is really worth looking at.

Basic hats—like berets, watch caps, and small-brim hats with shallow crowns—should not have ornamentation. Choose them for shape and color, and never forget that a hat, because it sits right on top of your face, must be in the most flattering shade imaginable. Here is another good area to try wearing those blusher shades; you may discover that the best one for you also works as a flattering accent to, and goes with, almost your entire wardrobe.

MISCELLANEOUS
Stockings

Every few years a great hullabaloo is made in the fashion press about textured or patterned stockings. Ignore it. Very few women look good in them, and they are a pain to coordinate as well as terrible looking on less-than-perfect legs. Stockings or pantyhose for a conservatively chic look should be either toned to your skin or toned to your shoes. In some cases, you can tone stockings to your skirt or dress rather than your shoes, but you will usually get a more flattering and lengthy line if leg and foot are sheathed in the same color. If you wear red or some other blazing color shoes, stick to skin-tone shades.

Buy stockings or pantyhose that hug your knees and ankles—nowadays there is no need for bagging with all the different stretch options available. For sportier looks, buy tights that match your shoes—try the sheer opaque rather than the opaque if you can find it. The former gives the leg a more shapely look.

Despite the fact that every list of fashion don'ts mentions it (and mine will, too), I continue to see many women who wear stockings with reinforced toes poking out of open-toe shoes and sandals. This looks truly terrible. If you constantly find yourself in this predicament because all your sandalfoot pantyhose have runs in them, buy *only* sandalfoot styles in the colors you need.

I have my reservations about knee-length stockings, too. I know they aren't supposed to show under pants, but if they happen to, they really look weird. Unless your pants are very dressy, they would be better complemented by knee socks or tights, anyway. And speaking of knee socks, if you are a grown woman, don't wear them under a skirt—such a look will never be conservative chic.

Vests

I feel that vests work in three situations: for very sporty occasions, in a somewhat casual office, or for a nonbusiness social activity. I think a woman in a conservative vested business suit looks as if she's wearing a costume—it's just too much.

Very busty women should steer clear of vests (especially the fitted ones) for any purpose, since they outline and call attention to the upper body. A woman with a very small bust usually looks very good in vests unless she is hippy (for the same reason—it outlines and calls attention to contrast between the upper body and the lower body). And a woman with a heavy waist or protruding stomach can use an open vest to blur the outline of those areas.

Choose a vest that is the right length for you. Long vests do not look good on hippy women with narrow shoulders. And very short vests do not look good on the long-waisted. Determine if you can wear the vest both open and closed. Also check whether a very fitted or a straight-cut version is more flattering, and what neckline is best.

Vests come in both woven and knitted fabrics, and can button up the front (which means you can wear them open or closed) or pull over the head.

For a lady who lunches, a vest may sometimes take the place of a jacket in a dressier ensemble. And a vest could go to work in an office as part of a somewhat casual outfit (with or without a jacket), provided the office is not extremely conservative.

If your sporty clothes are very muted in color, it can be fun to have one vest that is riotously colorful or highly patterned. Try a fuchsia vest with gray flannel pants and a gray shirt, or a red one with olive-green separates. Or,

MISCELLANEOUS

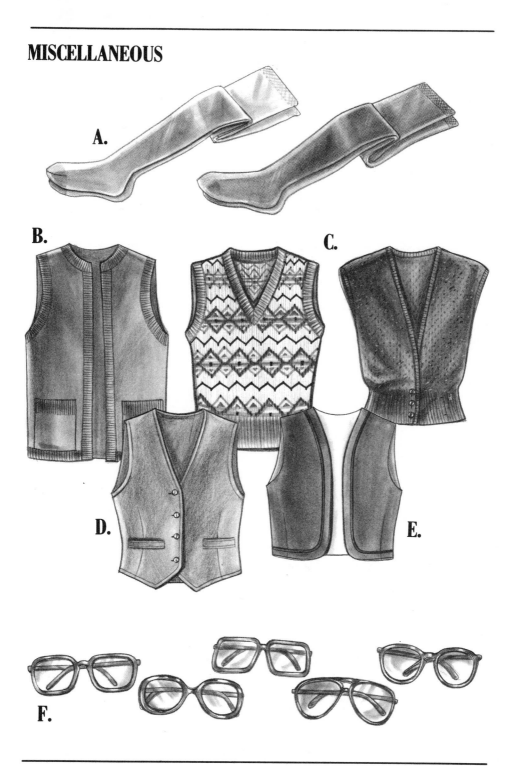

A: *Stockings and tights.* B: *Tabard.* C: *Sweater vests.* D: *Weskit.* E: *Bolero.* F: *Glasses.*

match a knitted vest exactly to what you are wearing, and let it just add texture. A vest worn for casual wear can have a little whimsy to it, such as an animal pattern, without adding an inordinately juvenile touch to your outfit, because it is a relatively small piece of clothing.

Glasses

Although the main purpose of glasses is not to be a fashion accessory, they are something you wear like any other accessory, and what's more, you wear them on your face. Because of the latter, color should be chosen with utmost care. And you can take one of two color directions: unobtrusive or frankly eye-catching. For an unobtrusive look, most women look best in some variety of tortoiseshell coloring. The dappled tortoiseshell pattern softens the color and blends in nicely with hair and brows. Tortoiseshell colors usually come in dark brown, honey, and sometimes a grayish brown. Dark-haired women usually look best in the dark or grayish brown, light-haired women in the honey, and gray-haired women in the grayish brown.

The other color route you can take is strong and obvious. Many women look good in red glasses or those that hit some part of the red spectrum (rose, brick, burgundy, etc.). First check what goes best with your coloring and personality; then consider how the glasses will work with your clothes.

Women's magazines are full of articles about how to choose the correct glasses shape for yourself, but I don't think they work very well. You can do better on your own if you are analytical about what you see.

The most basic consideration in the size and shape of your glasses is whether or not the top of them bisects your brow. Most women are more flattered by glasses that *do* bisect the brow, because, if they rise above or stop beneath the brow, they make you look as though you have four eyebrows. If your brows are not very dark, this may not be a problem, but it is hard for me to imagine any woman with dark and distinct eyebrows looking her best in any but brow-bisecting glasses.

If you don't look good in glasses that don't bisect your brow, you can immediately eliminate a great many styles.

Next, take a look at the bridge (the part that fits over your nose). Determine if you look best with a bridge that continues the line of the frame top or with one that drops beneath that line. If you have a prominent or sizeable nose, you may look better with the latter.

After you have the color, frame top, and bridge decided upon, devote your attention to the width, height, and shape of your frames—this is the hard part. Avoid complicated shapes (such as octagons), and look for the frames that seem most complimentary. If you find several that look good, stand up and check them out in a full-length mirror, if possible, just as you would any other accessory.

When you have found the best-looking frames, rethink every part of your look that will be affected by your glasses: makeup, hairstyle, jewelry, hats, scarves—whatever you wear on or near your face when you wear glasses. You may have to cut back on some of these if you wear glasses a lot and your accessories compete with them.

ACCESSORIES AS STATUS SYMBOLS

The status-symbol game is played out mostly in the accessories arena. Monogrammed shoes, scarves, jewelry, watches, and handbags are the pawns. And the prize is a feeling of security based on the fact that one recognizes and can afford to buy these talismans of the good life.

This is an adolescent attitude. Good taste is not the display of someone else's initials (or even the display of your own). As a matter of fact, a display of designer monograms reveals such an insecure sense of taste that it is a dead giveaway if someone truly sophisticated is sizing you up. Show confidence in your own taste by wearing what looks good on you and is appropriate to your life-style. Develop a signature look without a single signature on it. And leave the status items to the people who still haven't discovered the fact that it is all right to be an individual.

If you have a designer monogram accessory that you really like for itself, and you can't take off the monogram, just be sure you don't wear it with other monogrammed items—avoid monogram buildup.

HOW TO WEAR ACCESSORIES

After you have had some experience looking at and choosing accessories for yourself, you will no doubt notice that certain ones are much more flattering than others. Take advantage of this. If you see that berets look very good on you, buy several in different, but flattering, colors. Or buy slightly different versions of the same accessory in the same color and wear several of them together. If coral necklaces look nice on you, collect three different varieties in pink (or red): beads of smooth coral, unpolished irregularly shaped coral, and branch coral. That doesn't mean that, if you accumulate ten different red coral necklaces, you should wear them all together! Or buy two different black-and-white clip pins and wear them side by side on the neckline of a simple sweater.

Multiples of interesting and flattering jewelry have the effect of a collection—they show an element of consistent, and personal, taste.

You can also buy several of the same (or almost the same) accessory item in coordinating colors that are flattering to you and complement your wardrobe. Three scarves twisted into skinny tubes and looped around your neck together could look terrific at the throat of a shirt-style pullover sweater. Picture a gray sweater with pale gray, lavender, and peach scarves tucked into the open neck. Or wear three tiny bands of coral, jade, and ivory together on one finger.

When you are dressed and about to choose your accessories, decide first if one of them has priority. If you have only one pair of shoes that will go with your outfit, you should choose other accessories to work with them. Don't pick a jewelry look that is too dainty or heavy for the look of those shoes.

Build from the givens, but experiment, too. Try things together that you don't think will "go." Try accessories in unexpected places: a scarf as a belt, a cord belt as a necklace. Try unexpected combinations of accessories: precious and nonprecious jewelry together (gold bangles interspersed with wooden ones), a scarf and a necklace worn together. Wear an occasional unexpected color in an accessory: a brown silk shirt with matching brown gabardine pants and brown loaferish shoes worn with purple socks, a black shirtdress with jade and coral necklaces.

Decide where you wish to accessorize—just don't make it everywhere. Lots of necklaces may call for unobtrusive earrings and a ring instead of bracelets. Very sizeable or strong earrings may mean nothing else can be worn at the neck, and instead perhaps a strong-looking cuff bracelet might be worn to balance the look. A complicated belt or several belts worn together could mean skipping the necklaces. You don't want to look like a department store display counter! You want your accessories to subtly enhance and personalize your look.

When you look at your fully accessorized look—in your full-length mirror—don't hesitate to take off some (and, sometimes, all) of what you have put on. If you are willing to experiment, you are also willing to admit mistakes. You may look at it all and decide less is more, that you should try a totally new tack, or that you simply have on one piece too many.

If you try to be analytical about what is behind such errors, you may turn up very valuable general information about what looks good on you.

Some examples of how to accessorize conservatively chic clothing

Some examples of how to accessorize conservatively chic clothing

Some examples of how to accessorize conservatively chic clothing

ACCESSORIES CHECKLIST

General

1. Are you aware of what an accessory can do for you (harmonize with your shape and the shapes in your outfit, as well as with your coloring and the colors you wear, add interest, provide a focal point)?
2. Are you making the mistake of choosing your accessories solely on the basis of their intrinsic beauty, rather than for how they flatter you?
3. Are you checking the look of all accessories in a full-length mirror whenever possible?
4. Do you have a perspective on status-symbol accessories?
5. Do you know how to determine if one accessory has priority over others, how to wear multiples of the same accessory, how to make interesting and unexpected accessory combinations, where to position your accessories?

Shoes and Boots

1. Do you check to see that "your" size is indeed the right one for you in each pair of shoes? Do you try on both shoes?
2. Do you shop for shoes after you have spent some hours on your feet?
3. Do you think about whether summer and/or evening shoes would be more comfortable in a larger size?
4. Are you analytical about a shoe's symmetry, checking such things as how the heel joins the shoe and whether any straps are the right width?
5. Do you check both height and width of heels for their flattery to your legs—and your entire body?
6. Do you check heel and toe of open-back or open-toe shoes for proper fit?
7. If you wear open-toe shoes, are your feet well-groomed?
8. Do you really decide what color shoes will work with your clothes, or are you operating on the basis of "black looks right with everything" or some such misconception?
9. Are you shopping for a truly basic boot?

Handbags, Briefcases, Carryalls

1. Have you determined your own needs in this area?
2. Are you the weary owner of many bags—not one of which may be exactly right for you?
3. Would a shoulder bag or a clutch be better for your life-style?
4. What color is basic for your wardrobe?

Belts

1. Should you wear belts at all?
2. Do you recognize a basic belt in terms of width and buckle when you see one?
3. Do you think of the limitations of a belt with a jewelry buckle?
4. Are you aware that scarves, ties, etc. can also serve as belts?

Scarves and Shawls

1. Are you looking for the colors that are best for you?
2. Have you tried one or two flattering ways to tie scarves?
3. Are you buying scarves with the shapes that are easiest to deal with?
4. Are you better off with a square or rectangular shawl?
5. Have you thought of all the ways you might use a shawl—to add interest to separates or a dress, warmth to a coat or evening outfit?

Jewelry and Watches

1. Have you considered what style jewelry looks best on you (delicate, bold, etc.)?
2. Do you know where to place jewelry most effectively on your body?
3. Are you watching out for a too-matched-up look?
4. Are you watching out for a too-symmetrical look in tying scarves or wearing pins?
5. Are you aware of what shapes are most versatile in earrings?
6. What necklace length is best on you?
7. Do you know what shapes are most versatile in pins?
8. Have you tried accessorizing with pins rather than a necklace?
9. Can you spot which kinds of bracelets tend to be problematic?
10. Are you choosing a ring that is right for your style?
11. Are you picking the right kind of watch for your bone structure and life-style?

Hats and Gloves

1. Do you think about what you will wear your gloves with and whether or not you want their color to be an interesting accent?
2. Do you know what shape hats do not work with a conservatively chic look? What kind of hats do?
3. Have you experimented with the angle at which you wear a hat?

Stockings

1. Do you know why to skip textured stockings?
2. Do you know what to match the color of stockings or tights to?

Vests

1. Should you be wearing vests at all?
2. If you can wear a vest, would you look better in a longer or shorter one? A fitted or unfitted one?
3. Are you aware of how to use a vest as a colorful accent?

Glasses

1. Have you thought about what glasses colors will complement your hair and skin colors?
2. Are you thinking about whether or not the glasses shape flatters you? Does it bisect your brow? Is it too big or too small? Is the shape just too complicated?
3. After you have chosen your glasses, have you rethought your other accessories so that they do not compete with your glasses?

CHAPTER SEVEN

Underwear

You've now had a look at all the different pieces of clothing that go into a conservatively chic look, and a pretty thorough grounding in how to use the lines, colors, patterns, and textures of clothes to enhance your own looks.

Don't ruin everything by choosing the wrong underwear.

As with any other piece of clothing or accessory, it is not enough to find underwear that is pretty in and of itself. To be right for you, it should fit, flatter, and work for the clothes you will wear it under.

Lingerie for the boudoir can be purchased without regard to this last prerequisite (and there is nothing wrong with buying underwear solely for seductive purposes), but if you intend to wear it under your clothing as well, you have a number of things to think about.

Line

Underwear should enhance your lines and the lines of your clothing. To do this it has to fit correctly. Elastic that is so tight it digs into your skin produces ugly bulges that do nothing for your looks. Check the bottom and straps of your bra, the waist and legs of your underpants, and the waist of your pantyhose and half slip for over-snug fit. Have an eagle eye out for bikini-underpants bulge—unless you are built very straight from waist to hips (and sometimes even then), you are probably better off wearing briefs that come to the waist under knits and pants unless you like the look of that extra crease across your hips.

Some clothes have a better line if you wear either a half slip or full slip under them. Especially if you carry your weight in the hips and thighs, a noncling half slip in the proper length (never roll a slip at the waist to shorten it) should be one of the staples of your wardrobe. A noncling slip worn under knits not only keeps them from clinging to your every curve, it also performs some of the services of a girdle (it smooths your outline) with a lot less discomfort.

What about girdles and support briefs? I'm not a believer in them. I think your clothes should fit loosely enough (the conservative chic fit) so that you don't need them. You should feel and look comfortable in your clothes in order to look your best, and it's hard to feel that way when you're on the verge of a stomach ache from having your guts held together. Better to buy loose fitting clothes and to exercise regularly.

Forget about slips with slits in them—they never work. The slit in the slip simply refuses to line up with the slit in your skirt the moment you take a step. If you must wear slit skirts, either have them lined, try tap pants (wide-leg briefs) under them, or, if you are very slim, just wear pantyhose.

So that bra straps don't show out of certain necklines, you may need to invest in a strapless bra, or in lingerie straps to be sewn into the shoulder of your dress or blouse to hold the bra straps out of view. These are available in dime stores or at the notions counter in department stores.

If you are budgeted for minimal, basic underwear, do not buy anything with lace trim. You don't want the lace on your bra or your one and only half slip to show as funny lumps under a knit dress.

Color

Also, if you are budgeted for minimal, basic underwear, buy everything in the nude shade that is closest to your skin tone, and never touch anything in a print. Nude, not white, is the color that works under everything.

If you wear a lot of black and you have some black pieces that are loosely knit or sheer, it is the next color you should supply yourself with.

Special Underwear Needs

Now and then we all buy something unusual in cut and color, especially for dressing up. Be sure to think through your underwear needs whenever you purchase such an out-of-the-ordinary garment. Perhaps you will be better off with only pantyhose that has an opaque panty section under a very thin knit with slit skirt, so there will be no elastic line at your leg joint. Or you might need a nude body stocking under a very sheer dress.

It is worth a trip to the lingerie department when you buy such a piece of clothing to insure that the very (different) thing that captivated you about a garment does not turn out to be either a problem or an embarrassment. So, if specialized underwear is not within your budget, avoid all garments that require it.

CHAPTER EIGHT

Step Five: Coordination and Its Dividends

Coordination is something most women find easier to think about in its more limited aspects: "I need a pair of shoes to go with that red dress. . . . I could use another blouse or two for my tan suit. . . . I wonder if these pants will go with anything I already have . . . ?"

While coordination on this level is important, the real dividends come when it is practiced on a much grander scale—when it is applied to an entire wardrobe. It's true that this requires a good deal of organized thinking—but it can save you time, money, and a lot of anxiety.

What are coordination's dividends?

A Better Return for Your Money

I can't tell you how many times I have looked into a client's closet and seen a red dress, a blue dress, a yellow dress, a green dress, a purple dress, a brown dress, an orange dress, and a pink dress—and as many different color shoes and handbags. This is not a wardrobe; this is an assortment. It is also a waste of money. If you settle on the cuts and colors that look best on you, and buy your clothing in them, you won't need to spend all that money on accessories or on limited-use pieces.

If you have a tight budget, you must be very strict with yourself about not buying any colors or cuts that do not coordinate with your basic choices. Ideally, everything (or almost everything) should go with everything else.

If money is not a problem, you still want to get your money's *worth* from what you buy, and you won't get it from the odd item that only works with one skirt, or the pair of shoes that only goes with one dress. You may have the leeway to include more than one basic color or cut area in your wardrobe, but those different areas should still be well coordinated within themselves.

If you have a hard time disciplining yourself to be thoroughly coordinated, allow fewer restrictions in summer than in winter. Cold-weather clothes need to be more carefully coordinated because you layer more pieces together to keep warm. Summer can be less coordinated because you wear less! And, unless you live in a warm climate, cold weather lasts longer than warm.

Travel Benefits

To turn a well-coordinated wardrobe into a travel wardrobe, all you have to do is make sure your pieces aren't too bulky to pack well, and avoid pieces that crease readily. In every other respect, you already have a travel wardrobe.

The Outline of a Personal Style

One hears a lot about personal style and who has it, especially in relation to money. You can have money *and* have personal style, of course, but you can also have little money and lots of style.

Style is not just a matter of accumulation. *It is an ongoing process of selection.* And, in selecting, what one eliminates is often as or more important than what one includes. You can have the money to buy whatever appeals to you and have the information from all the previous chapters well in mind, but you still need to pull everything together into some kind of synthesis for yourself in order to have a style—and coordination is the tool for doing that.

Personal style is based on selectivity: this color rather than that one, this print rather than that one, this cut rather than that one. To have personal style, and to be coordinated, your shapes have to go together and your colors have to go together. Your choices—what you select, what you leave out—are a visual statement you make about yourself.

HOW TO COORDINATE SHAPES

As before, let's begin with cut. In Chapter Three, you got a look at what conservative cut is and information on what sorts of bodies each cut flatters. I hope you have experimented a bit by trying on some of these cuts and seeing how becoming they are to you. Now you want to put them together in a harmonious way that complements your own shape. The fact that so many garments are sold as "separates" today offers us wonderful freedom to make these combinations, but it also calls for a very good sense of proportion. If you don't have that sense of proportion now, you can develop it by being very aware of shape—your own and that of your clothes.

To help you relate one shape to another, here's a garment-by-garment rundown of cut-related factors to keep in mind when shopping.

Coats

Did you ever stop to think that many people never see you in anything else? This is a very important, and expensive, purchase.

Before we go any further, consider the primary function of a coat: to keep you warm. It is the fabric *and the cut* of a coat that keep you warm. If you are shopping for one coat, you must find one that accomplishes this task all by itself—or you must be able to wear other layers under it. Otherwise, you will need a wardrobe of coats.

Other than the warmth of the fabric, what cut-related features contribute to how warm you will be in a coat? Length is one. A longer coat is warmer than a shorter one. How the neck is cut is another. The warmest coats close snugly at the neck, and a collar (especially if you can turn it up) provides an additional source of warmth. Sleeves that come in at the wrist are warmer than loose ones.

The colder you tend to get, the more seriously you must consider these factors.

Suppose you are only going to get one coat, and it must work with (and for) everything. You want it to work for late fall, winter, and early spring weather, for everything from fairly casual to fairly dressed up occasions. What is the best all-purpose coat to buy?

The best all-purpose coat is a steamer . . . which also happens to be the coat that looks best on most women. It should fit well in the shoulders, but the body should be loose to quite full, the sleeves fairly wide and loose at the wrist, and the neck should close snugly. Most women look best in a collar that is not too large.

Buy this coat long for two reasons: first, you want it to cover the longest as well as the shortest skirt or dress in your wardrobe; second, length gives the steamer sweep and balances the fullness (short versions look square and bulky). And if you want a steamer with a belt, you should buy the coat long enough so that the belt does not make it either boxy or too short for your wardrobe.

Although loose sleeves are not your warmest option, they enable the steamer to fit over everything, including suit jackets and heavy sweaters. You need this versatility if you only have one coat.

Always consider what you will be wearing under your coat. Check carefully length, body width, sleeve width, armhole depth, and the neck, no matter what style you purchase. You don't want your coat to look like a sausage casing.

What about how your coat looks open? Again, many people will see you this way, so be sure your coat has this versatility. Coats with asymmetrical closings almost never look good open, no matter how elegant they may look closed.

If your coat has shoulder pads, think about what other garments with shoulder pads will be worn underneath. If you wear a blouse with shoulder pads under a jacket with them under a coat with them, you will get quite a

A: *A steamer coat fits well over layers.* B: *The reefer looks best over fewer layers.*

The cape can be casual . . .   or dressy.

buildup! If you like shoulder pads in blouses and jackets, perhaps your coat should not have them.

The reefer, because it is a very tailored style, looks good over trousers, slim skirts, turtleneck sweaters, tailored shirts, lightweight tailored suits, and slim dresses. If you can buy only one coat, this is not the coat to buy—unless your entire wardrobe is made up of narrowly cut pieces and you are not terribly bothered by cold. It's hard to layer a sweater and jacket under a reefer without its losing the slim look that is its raison d'être. This coat will only take you into dressier occasions if your dressy style is also very tailored.

A cape looks elegant with an enormous range of clothing cuts. It is just as wonderful over pants and a sweater as it is over a very feminine dress. And nothing makes a more elegant evening coat. However, it has limitations—it is seasonal and it makes it difficult to carry things. If you live in a climate where it gets chilly but never terribly cold, you really should consider one. And if you do consider one, your two main decisions will be how long to buy it and whether or not to get one with arm slits. Like the steamer, it should be on the long side—it will have more sweep and drama and will fit over more things. With arm slits, you can have buttons up the front, which make the cape a bit warmer (although wind can still make its way up the slits). Without them, the cape is even more dramatic.

Handy as a trenchcoat is for some, it is not a rainy-day solution for everyone. As I stated in the chapter on cut, the classic trenchcoat style looks great on some women and terrible on many others. If it is not becoming to you, consider a raincoat cut in another conservative style. And consider, also, whether or not a raincoat is your best bet. You might be better served by an umbrella and a lightweight wool spring coat, or, for out-and-out downpours that occur on the way to anything but the most conservative office or the most dressed-up occasion, by a slicker with matching rain hat (not a plastic scarf). If you do choose a trenchcoat, remember that it, like the reefer, is basically a tailored look; thus you will get more mileage out of it if this is the way you dress. Here again, a steamer-style raincoat would cover a wider range of cuts more successfully.

A princess-style coat can look very elegant, very feminine, but it is even more limited in scope than a reefer. This is a coat for a lady-who-lunches, who can afford to own more than one coat. It accommodates fuller skirts very nicely, but its fitted waist precludes any but the lightest clothing from the waist up. It works better with dresses than with sportswear, and it might make a good dress coat.

And that is just about it for conservatively cut coats, with the exception of kimono or bathrobe styles, which lie between the steamer and the reefer in versatility. They can be a bit dressier than the reefer and may be cut a bit fuller, which gives you more freedom in what you can wear under them. Many bathrobe-style coats come with shawl collars, which are very graceful, but check to see if they conflict with the necklines of everything you wear underneath.

The main thing that troubles me about bathrobe and indeed all wrap-style coats is the sash. Unlike the steamer, which often comes with an optional sash, wrap-style coats depend on sashes to hold them closed. The strong vertical formed by the sash ends as they fall from the knot is frequently cited in other books as a slimming line. I'm not so sure . . . and even if that's so, what you gain in apparent slimness you may lose in sleekness if the dangling sash ends add a needless complication to your line. Picture the dangling sash with a dangling shoulder bag—it's too much dangle . . . too much detail where you don't need it.

Outerwear Jackets

An outerwear jacket may be a heavier version of any of the jackets discussed in Chapter Three. Consider the same factors in choosing one as you would for the purchase of a coat or a suit (lighter-weight) jacket.

Length is as crucial in an outerwear jacket as it is for any other kind of jacket. And many outerwear jackets, for the sake of warmth, cover the entire hip area, and often much of the thigh. If such a long jacket is unbecoming to you in a lighter weight, it may be even more so in a heavier fabric—unless you wear it only with pants. Do you find you look heavier in an outerwear jacket than in a coat? Boxier? Shorter-legged? Check jacket length and squareness if you do.

Perhaps you are using an outerwear jacket instead of a coat? This is a risky endeavor. A coat is a much more versatile garment in terms of what you can wear under it. And, in the looks department, a coat's heaviness of fabric is balanced by its basically rectangular shape (longer, thus slimmer, than it is wide), while an outerwear jacket comes out as a heavy square. Any tendency *you* have to look like a heavy square will be reinforced by the jacket more than by the coat.

Low pockets on a longish outerwear jacket can be particularly unflattering, especially square patch pockets. And beware of the outerwear jacket that looks like a chopped-off coat, which many do.

If your outerwear jacket has lapels, how do they look with what the lapels frame underneath? If you buy a jacket that closes to the neck, you don't have to worry about this.

Four ways to wear a shirtdress

Dresses

You have two major concerns in relating your dress shapes to the rest of your wardrobe. First, you must consider how the cut of your dresses will work with the outerwear garments you may need to wear over them for warmth. (Obviously, this will not be as big a consideration in summer or in a warm climate.) When you open your coat or outerwear jacket, the dress underneath should look right with it—they should look as if they were meant to be worn together. Then, if you want to be able to wear your dress under a jacket for a more businesslike or authoritative look, you must make sure that it will fit comfortably under the jacket you have in mind, and that the shapes will look good together. You should not buy a dress that is too long for your coat, or has too full a skirt to fit comfortably under it. And a dolman sleeve can be a particular problem in a coat or jacket with a high armhole—it needs a deep armhole or a cape.

The dolman dress is a rather obvious example of a shape that will only fit comfortably under certain other shapes. Other pairings may fit together physically yet be less than pleasing aesthetically.

You can wear a shirtdress with any conservatively cut coat in the sense that it will fit under any style we have mentioned, but it will look odd paired with a princess coat or a cape unless the dress is a formal-looking collarless version that buttons to the neck, or has a Peter Pan collar. Except for dressmaker jackets or blouse-jackets, which are ordinarily worn on their own anyway, you can wear a shirtdress that opens at the neck with any conservatively cut jacket except the jewel-neck cardigan jacket. You can wear your Peter Pan collar shirtdress with a jewel-neck cardigan jacket, but a shirtdress with conventional open neck or lapels will need a cardigan jacket with a V neck. And the same goes for cardigan sweaters or sweater-jackets.

A V-neck vest (pullover or button variety) complements the lines of a conventional shirtdress, and a shirtdress in a fairly weighty fabric (like wool) can sometimes be worn with a lightweight wool or cotton turtleneck underneath.

Two-piece dresses that look like conventional shirtdresses can be worn in the same pairings as the latter, provided you wear the shirt tucked into the skirt. A two-piece dress in a weightier wool or cotton that is worn with the top as an overblouse often does not need, or look right with, a jacket. Because the overtop has more of the feeling of a jacket, such a dress will pair better with a coat—but probably not with a princess coat, which may be too fitted and dressy for it.

Because it is actually a blouse and skirt, the two-piece dress should be analyzed not only as a dress but also as a blouse and skirt, so that it coordinates happily with the other skirts and blouses in your wardrobe.

The coatdress also does not need a jacket—it is important enough to stand on its own. If you feel the need of one to supply warmth, stick to a V-neck cardigan jacket or sweater. And wear the coatdress with a steamer or wrap-style coat—a coatdress under a reefer might look oddly like two coats.

A bathrobe-style wrap dress under a bathrobe-style wrap coat will look like two coats, as well. Try a steamer or a cape, and stick to an unconstructed, loose-fitting shawl-collar jacket if you need one with the dress.

The basic blouson works with all coats, all jackets, and a tabard or bolero vest. So does a sweater dress, which you may also be able to pair with a V-neck pullover as well as any of the vests.

Jackets

This is a very important area, and fraught with pitfalls. A good jacket, especially a highly tailored one, can be a rather expensive purchase, as I have already noted. To justify its price, it should be very versatile.

Let's begin with the blazer, which, as I have said before, is what many women think of when they think of a jacket. In the chapter on cut, I voiced my reservations about how flattering this style is to many women who insist on buying it. Assuming that it is flattering to your own shape, your next decision is whether to buy a constructed (closely fitted and highly shaped) or unconstructed (looser fitting, squarer in the torso, and often unlined) style. If you want a very shaped and formal look, a constructed blazer is better. If you like the option of wearing your jacket belted—and if the jacket is on the long side, belting it may give it a better proportion—you will be better off with an unconstructed style.

Look at the length of the jacket and decide if it works with the length and shapes of your skirts. A very long jacket with a rather short skirt is only for the very tall or long-legged; an awful lot of leg must hang from that skirt to balance the long-torso look of a long jacket. Look to see how your jackets line up with such detail on the upper part of the skirt as pockets, pleats, etc. Try on jackets with single, double, and no vents to see what flatters your body and skirt styles most. In general, the ventless blazers are more versatile and hide extra weight better.

If you are considering a rather fitted blazer, think about how fitted the waist should be—will you wear a heavy sweater under it or just a silk blouse? And how much do you want to emphasize your waist? Check the blazer's lapels and think about how they will look with the blouses or shirts you intend to wear

A: *Shawl collars look graceful together.* B: *A tie-neck dress looks pretty with a Chanel-style jacket.* C: *A sweater dress with a sweater-jacket.*

A: *A longer, fitted blazer with trousers.* B: *An unconstructed, medium-length blazer with a straight skirt (note how the collars work together).* C: *A short, fitted, very feminine blazer with a fuller skirt.*

under them. And, if you are tempted by a double-breasted style, remember that these look peculiar unbuttoned.

The longer and more fitted the jacket, the better it looks with straighter skirts. Blazers—especially the longer, more fitted ones—look better with straighter rather than fuller skirts. So do the longer shawl-collar jackets, unless they are unshaped enough so that you can belt and blouse them to a shorter length. Skirt fullness looks odd poufing out halfway down the thigh; and a jacket that is long and fitted in the hips will not accommodate such fullness. Any jacket that doesn't descend much below the top of the hipbone will look fine with a fuller skirt.

Check to see how the shawl-collar jacket works with your shirt collars—it may line up strangely with shirts that have notched lapels and do not button to the neck. You are safe with most shirts that button to the neck, a shawl-collar blouse, a tie-neck blouse, or a back-button style with jewel neckline.

Cardigan or Chanel jackets don't work with shirts, unless the shirts button to the neck and have Peter Pan collars. You need the V-neck variation of this jacket if you intend to wear it with common garden-variety shirts. Tie-neck blouses, blouses with jewel or square necklines, pullovers, and turtlenecks all work well with cardigan jackets. The shorter cardigans look great with fuller or slimmer skirts, and a jacket of this type in any length will be no problem with pants or trousers.

A kimono-cut cardigan jacket with mandarin collar and no buttons or other closing is a very versatile piece to have in a soft fabric such as mohair or wool melton. Its loose shape looks fine open over pants and even quite full skirts, but you can also wrap, belt, and blouse it for a different look.

When looking for an unconstructed shirt-jacket, consider an overblouse style that pulls over the head as well as the more standard shirt-style jacket. Unless you are wearing them with pants, all shirt-jackets generally look their best belted and bloused. Avoid shirttails for a cleaner and more flattering line. You can wear a shirt-jacket successfully over most sweaters and tailored shirts. But the safari shirt-jacket, with all those pockets and epaulets, may be too much detail for you.

The fitted, somewhat dressy, dressmaker jacket is usually worn on its own, but occasionally it works with a jewel-neck blouse or lightweight sweater underneath. It coordinates well with either full or straight skirts, but not with wrap-style skirts.

The blouse-jacket handles much the same as the dressmaker jacket, but the skirts it will work with depend on the style of blouse-jacket you end up with. Check the sections on the jacket or blouse it most closely resembles.

A: *A Chanel-style jacket with a Peter-Pan-collar shirt.*
B: *A short Chanel-style jacket with a fuller skirt.*

A. A shawl-collar jacket blouses slightly over a fuller skirt. B: A *mandarin collar on a longer Chanel-style jacket.*

A convertible kimono jacket over a fuller, more casual skirt . . . and wrapped and belted to echo the line of an elegant wrap skirt

A: *A shirt-jacket.*   B: *A pullover shirt-jacket.*

A: *A dressmaker jacket and a non-matching skirt — a suit alternative.* B: *Two uses of that versatile hybrid, the blouse-jacket.*

General checkpoints for any jacket are:

1. Length. Does it flatter you? Does it work with your skirts or pants?

2. Armhole depth. Will you be wearing a heavy sweater underneath or a dolman or batwing cut?

3. Collar or lapel size and shape. Are these in the proper scale for you? Do they coordinate with blouse and sweater necklines?

Beware additional extraneous detail—it impedes coordination. Avoid many or prominent pockets, ornate buttons, tabs, and epaulets. If the jacket comes with a belt, don't feel you have to retain the riders that hold it in place—they may be unsightly or in the wrong place for you. Never wear a short-sleeve jacket over a long-sleeve blouse or sweater. And never buy a jacket that doesn't fit when you button it, even if you usually wear it open to hide a thick waist. Remember—a good jacket is one that you can wear open or closed!

Skirts

Since a jacket is usually a more expensive purchase than a skirt, it is often better to buy the jacket first, then look for skirts to coordinate with it. This will actually help you to make the best skirt choices by narrowing the field; you'll be looking for a skirt shape that flatters you and looks good with your jacket(s).

Although straight skirts and some of the straighter dirndls make special demands on your figure, they are the easiest to coordinate with jacket shapes: A straight skirt or straight dirndl can be worn with any of the conservatively cut jackets, including the dressmaker jacket and the blouse-jacket. The fuller dirndl, however, won't look good with a longer jacket (particularly if you button or close it), because it will look as if it is bursting out of the jacket. Pick shorter, more fitted jacket styles for these skirts.

I like A-line skirts best with belted jackets or jackets that have a definite waistline, like fitted blazers and dressmaker styles.

Wrap skirts are a special problem to coordinate. While the strong vertical line of the overlap can be slimming and lengthening, it is a complication in the skirt's line that limits its compatibility with jackets and blouses. If you wear such a skirt, consider the line of the overlap a focal point, and pick jackets, blouses, and sweaters that either echo it or do not compete with it. A double-breasted jacket with a closing that lines up with the skirt overlap, a surplice-wrap blouse or sweater that forms a diagonal from the skirt overlap to

A: *A back-button blouse does not compete with a pleated skirt.* B: *A full skirt works with a short sweater.* C: *A longer sweater slides gracefully over sewn-down pleats.*

the opposite shoulder, any pullover shirt-jacket or shirt-style sweater, or a back-button blouse will show off a slim wrap skirt to its best advantage.

Circular skirts work best with jackets, sweaters, and sweater-jackets that end at or just below the waistline, or that come in at the waist and flare in a brief peplum over the hips. Try dressmaker jackets, belted shirt-jackets, the shorter cardigan jackets, belted sweater jackets that are not too long, and shortish pullover sweaters that blouse slightly above the waistband. A rather full skirt needs the look of a definite waist to keep it from looking shapeless, but you may want to balance its fullness with a certain amount of fullness above the waist: a loosely bloused pullover, a peasant blouse, small shoulder pads and a slight puff to add fullness to the shoulders of a dressmaker jacket—anything but a tightly fitted look, since that will make you look bottom-heavy.

If pleated skirts look good on you, they will look good with any of the conservative jacket shapes. However, if the pleats are sewn down, the jacket should cover the entire sewn-down area—otherwise you will have an ill-matched look. Sweaters or blouses worn with a skirt that has sewn-down pleats should either tuck into the waist with no bunchiness, extend to cover the sewn-down portion, or stop just below the waist. Skirts with pleats that release from the waistband offer fewer coordinating restrictions—but they add weight and are harder to wear.

Check skirt length for proportion with jackets, sweaters, and overblouses. Examine pockets critically as potential line-clutterers or hip or seat emphasizers. Pay attention to how the skirt closes: side or back zipper, front placket, button front, front or back wrap, etc. Ideally, the closing should not be a focal point—button-front skirts can look very busy with button-front shirts or jackets. And waist detail, such as sewn-on partial belts, doesn't coordinate well, either.

Pants

Once you have determined which (if any) pants look best on you, you need to decide how long to make them. And to make that decision, you need to know the heel height of the shoes you will be wearing the pants with—something of a problem if you like to wear shoes of different heights with your pants.

There is one way to solve this common dilemma, but it will not work for the short-legged: Make all of your pants ankle-length, which will enable you to wear them with shoes of any height. If you like to wear very beautiful or highly styled shoes, this length will inevitably show them off; or you can wear simpler shoes with highly patterned or colorful socks or stockings (this is the one exception to the no-textured-stocking rule, because so little of it peeks out here). This focus on shoes and socks or stockings works best if you keep sweaters, blouses, and jackets very simple in line and, possibly, color.

For those with shorter legs or those who have less interest in concentrating their pants looks on ankles and feet, determine first which shoes you will wear with your pants—moccasins and heavier pumps or spectators are best unless you are going for a rather dressy look—then have your pants hemmed so that they break slightly over the front of the shoe. Very narrow-leg pants should be a bit shorter than wider-leg ones.

Many women who wear pants feel that a jacket must cover the entire seat, especially if they are heavy in that area. If you have this problem you should, of course, question if pants are the best choice for you. Don't reach for a long jacket for pants by rote—many short jackets look wonderful with pants, and you may actually look slimmer in such a combination, especially if you have been wearing jackets that are so long they hang below your seat and foreshorten your legs. However, since pants give the leg a longer line than skirts, a jacket bought solely to wear with pants can often be a bit longer than one that must also go with skirts.

Just about any jacket style, cardigan, sweater-jacket, or overblouse can look good with pants if it flatters you in the crucial seat area. If you look basically okay in pants but feel a bit bottom-heavy, balance weight in hips and thighs with a little bulk on top: a pullover in a thick and crunchy weave, a roomy overshirt, a square-cut rather than midriff-fitted jacket, small shoulder pads, drop shoulders (to extend the shoulder line), etc.

Cuffed pants or trousers are foreshortening and have a busy line—they are for the long-legged, and they sharply limit the amount of other detail in your outfit. And culottes take well to the jackets and short, blousy sweaters that work with the fuller dirndls—which they resemble in front.

Blouses and Shirts

The focal point of a blouse or shirt is usually the neckline, and if you intend to wear your blouses under jackets, be sure that the necklines of both of them coordinate well together. If you are buying a tailored shirt, be aware of whether or not it has a stand collar. Check if a stand collar looks right on you, and how it looks under and over your jacket neckline. If you wear your tailored shirts open at the neck with the shirt lapels on top of the jacket lapels, make sure that these line up well, and check that the underside of the shirt neckline is finished neatly enough to be worn unbuttoned.

As I mentioned in the skirt section, be very wary of combining a jacket, a shirt, and a skirt that all button up the front. Such a combination can look too

A. *How to wear ankle pants.* B: *Longer, unbelted overblouses tend to look best with pants.*

busy—and too vertical. If, for instance, you have narrow shoulders and fairly wide hips, you might want to emphasize more of a horizontal in the upper part of your outfit—a pullover under the jacket, or an overblouse instead of a jacket, might accomplish more for you (even if the skirt doesn't button up the front, this may work better for you).

Again, as previously mentioned, if you like shoulder pads, watch for too much buildup if you wear them in both blouse and jacket or sweater. Shoulders that are too elevated have a tense look about them.

Fullness in the body and in the sleeve should be checked if you wear a blouse under a jacket or sweater. And length of the blouse is very important if you want to wear it as an overblouse. Steeply cut shirttails do not look good worn outside—choose those with a more gradual curve or, better yet, a straight-cut bottom. A very long overblouse may make a rather short skirt look awkward, unless you are very tall or long-legged. Of course, you could take up some of the length by belting and blousing it, or you might leave it unbelted and wear it with pants. The hippy should also avoid very long overblouses that stop just at their widest point—shorter is usually better.

You can wear a tailored shirt with any of the conservative skirt shapes, but for the most unfussy and elegant look, choose one with covered buttons or a placket that conceals the buttons completely. Such a shirt will coordinate better with a wrap skirt—or any other skirt with prominent detail. Again, remember that covered buttons or concealed ones do not detract from jewelry.

A back-closing blouse, as I mentioned in the skirt section, works well with wrap skirts because it doesn't compete with the line of the (front) wrap. It works with all the other conservative skirt shapes, too, and is often an excellent troubleshooter when skirts or pants have pocket flaps, contrasting trim, or other salient details that require a quiet look on top.

Tie-neck and shawl-collar blouses also work with all the skirt shapes as well as with pants and trousers. But peasant blouses look best with skirts or pants with some fullness: dirndls, straight dirndls, circular skirts, or pants with a little shirring at the waist.

Keep a particularly sharp eye on balance when you wear a blouse and skirt (or pants) without a jacket, cardigan, or vest. A blouse that is less than perfect in the balance department may work perfectly so long as you wear it under a jacket or other top layer that provides the balance you need in the upper body. But when you wear a blouse on its own, it must balance the skirt or pants on its own. If you are smaller on top, use blouse fullness, extended shoulders or cap sleeves, drop shoulders, boat necks—whatever you can muster—to balance hip or thigh fullness. And if you are top-heavy, stick to (modestly) open neck-

A: *Balance hip fullness with full sleeves . . . or extended shoulders.*
B: *A belted overblouse gives a more dressed look to pants.*

lines that give a V effect, such as open shirt collars, shawl necklines, and surplice-wrap styles.

Sweaters

Pullover sweaters should be subject to the same criteria as shirts and blouses, cardigans to the same criteria as jackets in terms of fullness, length, and neckline. However, you'll sometimes wear a cardigan closed without anything under it, or a pullover on top of another layer.

If a conservative chic look is your aim, avoid preppy or schoolgirlish sweater looks. A perfectly simple jewel-neck pullover with matching cardigan can look very sophisticated, but a Shetland crew-neck sweater over a tailored shirt looks juvenile. However, a Shetland sweater worn on its own with a well-cut skirt and an interesting belt is something else again. And a shirt layered under a pullover that has a shirt collar can look very nice.

A well-cut turtleneck will go with just about any skirt, pants, or jacket shape. In recent years, cowl necks have often been easier to find than turtlenecks, but they are by no means as versatile—make sure the cowl neck works under the jackets you'll wear such sweaters with.

Jewel-neck pullovers also work with any style skirt, pants, or jacket. A V-neck pullover is more limited. It looks fine on its own with pants or trousers, or with a straight or A-line skirt. And you can add a shirt underneath it to all of these combinations. But it looks too busy with the other skirt shapes, and it doesn't line up that well with jacket necklines.

V-neck cardigans, too, accommodate shirts well, but look odd with the necklines of other blouses. Try a jewel-neck cardigan with those.

A medium-length sweater-jacket cut like a jewel-neck cardigan, but with no buttons or closing and enough overlap to wrap, is one of the world's most versatile garments. It can be worn belted closed or loosely open over all kinds of blouses, sweaters, and dresses, and can be worn by itself, belted, with a good-looking pin to secure the bustline (unless you are very busty). If you buy it on the short side, it should work with just about every skirt shape, including the front wrap (if you wrap it, it echoes the wrap in the skirt).

If most of your wardrobe is made up of simple shapes, you not only make coordination easier, you also provide a setting that will showcase you and the occasional garment or accessory to which you wish to draw attention because it truly flatters you. To see how this works, read the section on focus at the end of the chapter.

A: A shorter sweater set pairs with culottes. B: A shirt-style sweater — more grown-up than a shetland over a blouse.

A convertible sweater-jacket worn as a jacket over trousers . . . and as a wrap top with a skirt

HOW TO COORDINATE COLORS

In Chapter Four, you experimented freely with color combinations, considered whether you look best in monochromatic, high-contrast, or low-contrast combinations, and learned what colors look good near your face. Now you are going to take the leap from coordinating single outfits to organizing a season's worth of clothes.

How to begin? Don't be overwhelmed by the scale of it. Start with your most flattering color (or one that is appropriate to your life-style) and begin to use it with a lavish hand. If you look best in black, invest heavily in it. If tan always looks good on you, make it that, but be sure the shade of tan is right. Of course, if the most beautiful color in the world on you is pinkish mauve, and you work in a Wall Street law firm, you will have to set limits on your enthusiasm. A mauve wool suit and a mauve coat are not appropriate in a very conservative firm, although mauve blouses and mauve scarves might be worn there.

Assuming that your best color is one that is appropriate to your life-style, it becomes your "neutral," whether it is truly a neutral or not. It *is* a neutral in the sense that whatever other colors you buy must relate to it. Buy your coat in it, a good suit, a pair of pants, a simple dress (or two-piece dress), and possibly shoes and a bag.

If a monochromatic look is most flattering to you, you can buy virtually all your major pieces in your neutral, adding color only through accessories. If a low-contrast look is your best bet, add pieces in other colors but with similar color depth and intensity. If a high-contrast look is most becoming, add pieces in other light, medium, and dark tones. And if you look good in all of these, add pieces that allow you a little of each type of combination.

For instance, if black is your neutral, buy other black pieces for an outfit or two with a monochromatic look. Add interest through textural variety, scarves, and jewelry. For a low-contrast look, combine black with very dark burgundy, hunter green, or teal blue. For a high-contrast look, combine black with tan, white, red, or mauve. Choose patterned pieces with black backgrounds, or black outlines.

If your basic color is tan, buy other tan pieces for a monochromatic look (make sure they all work well together), again using textural interest and accessories to give variety. For a low-contrast look, combine tan with gray, army green, or light blue. For a high-contrast look, combine tan with black, burgundy, or red.

Whenever you add a color to your mix, try to choose one that works not just with the "neutral," but with the others, too. If you do, you will get the greatest number of combinations.

Although total coordination is something to shoot for in theory, it does not always work out perfectly in practice for one very good reason: Some combinations look better on you than others, no matter how well the colors work together. Why is this? Often it is because certain combinations are more figure-flattering than others. If you own a black suit and a white suit, both of which look wonderful on you, and both of which are identical in shape, you may find, if you are narrower above than below the waist, that the white jacket over the black skirt looks better than the black jacket over the white skirt. Such is life; but you still have three good combinations.

Remember when choosing your pieces that those worn near your face must be in your most flattering colors. Don't just choose color to go with other color; choose it to go with you, too.

If you tan readily, you may find that your summer "neutral" is different from your winter one. If it is, you will have more of a feeling of seasonal variety, because your warm weather clothes may be in very different colors from your cold weather ones. But if your neutral doesn't vary, you may be able to use some pieces from your summer wardrobe with your winter wardrobe, as well.

Build around your neutral by choosing pieces that will take it in different color directions. Add pieces over a period of years. And only begin a totally different neutral if your initial one is already very extensively coordinated.

Here is a checklist to help you shop for color, by garment.

Coats

1. Because a coat is worn near your face, it should be in a very flattering color.

2. Depending on your life-style, a coat may need to be in a color that doesn't soil too readily.

3. A coat should be in a color that coordinates with everything you will wear under it.

4. There should be a very good reason for buying a coat in a pattern rather than a solid.

5. There should be a very good reason for buying a coat with contrasting trim, since that will severely limit its versatility.

Dresses

1. Because a dress is worn near your face, it should be in a very flattering color.

2. Choose a dress in a color that will coordinate with your coat and any jackets you will want to wear it with.

3. If you buy a dress with a pattern, be sure that the background color is flattering and appropriate.

4. There should be a good reason for buying a dress with contrasting trim.

Jackets

1. Because a jacket is worn near your face, it should be in a very flattering color.

2. Your jacket should coordinate well with every other piece you wish to wear it with, including your coat.

3. If your figure is top- or bottom-heavy, try to balance that by choosing a jacket in a dark shade if you are top-heavy or in a light shade if you are bottom-heavy.

4. There should be a very good reason for buying a jacket with contrasting trim.

Skirts

1. Because a skirt is not next to your face, you may choose a color that is not totally flattering.

2. If your figure needs help, choose a skirt in a color that will help give it balance.

3. Choose a skirt in a color that will go with everything else you will want to wear it with, including your coat.

4. A skirt may need to be in a color that is more soil-resistant than some of your other garments.

5. There should be a very good reason for buying a skirt with contrasting trim.

Pants

1. Because pants are not next to your face, you may choose a color that is not totally flattering.

2. If your figure needs help, choose pants in a color that will help give it balance.

3. Choose pants in a color that will go with everything else you will want to wear them with, including your coat.

4. Pants may need to be in a color that is more soil-resistant than some of your other garments.

Blouses and Shirts

1. Because a blouse is worn near your face, it should be in a very flattering color.

2. If your figure needs help, choose a blouse in a color that will help give it balance, especially if you will not be wearing a jacket or sweater over it.

3. Choose a blouse in a color that will go with everything else you will want to wear it with, including your coat.

Sweaters

1. Because a sweater is worn near your face, it should be in a very flattering color.

2. If your figure needs help, choose a sweater in a color that will help give it balance, especially if you will not be wearing a jacket or sweater over it.

3. Choose a sweater in a color that will go with everything else you will want to wear it with, including your coat.

FOCUS

With both cut and color coordinated on the level of both wardrobe and individual outfit, there is one final element in a conservative chic look for which you must muster your powers of selection: focus.

We have already spent some time looking at focus in the accessories chapter, when we considered how accessories can help add a focal point to an outfit.

Why do we need a focal point? Because the human eye can only take in, and make sense of, so much at one time. If you present the eye with an outfit where everything is of the same complexity, the same level of interest, nothing stands out and no impression is made. If you load yourself down with too much detail, none of it will make an impression. It is up to you to decide what you want people to look at, what you want people to focus on, when they look at you.

Although accessories are an easy way of providing a focal point for an outfit, there are other possibilities. You can get people to focus on shape, color, pattern, texture, your face, or some other part of your body. But in order to do that, you have to really feature what you want them to focus on by downplaying all the other focal possibilities.

You can get people to focus on your face by framing it with flattering jewelry and color—and leaving the rest of your look very simple. You can draw all eyes to your waist by wearing a very fitted and eye-catching (in color or cut) belt, and by providing no competition for that belt in the rest of your outfit. You can focus on shape by wearing one that is very important-looking (like a dolman dress) and keeping all the other elements of your outfit unobtrusive. And you can draw people's eyes to color, pattern, or texture, by providing strong interest in those areas and little competition elsewhere.

The important thing about a focal point is that there be only one. And you can work with the same one throughout your entire wardrobe (focal interest only in shoes), or you can vary it depending on what you feel like featuring (shoes one day, jewelry the second, a strong pattern the third, and luscious texture the fourth). You may already be doing this unconsciously. If not, try a conscious approach: Decide what you want to call attention to, feature it, and keep everything else very simple.

CHAPTER NINE

Grooming and Clothing Care

Y ou cannot be chic—conservative or otherwise—without good grooming, so it is very important to be honest about the time and attention you have to spend on yourself and your clothing. No matter how terrific the hairstyle, if you have neither the time nor the dexterity to keep it up, and you lack the money to have the hairdresser handle it for you, it becomes a liability. Polished fingernails can give a very finished look to your appearance, but chipped fingernail polish is a worse liability than none at all. A beautiful, crisp-looking linen suit is elegant summer dressing—if someone irons it each time you wear it.

Know the limits of your time, money, and energy, and make things easy for yourself wherever you can. A wash-and-wear hairdo that makes full use of your hair's natural tendencies is usually more becoming than a studied one, anyway. Cleanliness, a becoming cut, and unfettered movement (unless you wear your long hair up) are the things to strive for in any hairstyle.

Cleanliness and good grooming are a commitment you make to yourself and your looks, and any commitment requires upkeep time.

If you pluck your eyebrows for a better shape, have a regular schedule of eyebrow care. If you polish fingernails and/or toenails, never let polish get chipped or messy. And if you don't have time to polish fingernails regularly, file and buff them instead. If you bleach facial hair, don't wait too long between bleachings; and if you wear sheer stockings, don't wait too long to shave your legs.

I'm sure you already know a great deal about personal cleanliness and grooming, and there are always plenty of magazine articles to cover this ongoing aspect of daily life. So let me direct your attention here to the clothing aspect of grooming, which sometimes gets shorter shrift in the press.

When you put your clothes away at the end of a season, or when you take them out at the beginning of one, is a good time to give them the once-over for potential problems. Recheck fit and all finishing details. Are buttons missing? Replace them in the right color, and with the right color thread. Check the linings of all lined garments for droop and rehem if necessary. Check the side seams on knit garments for droop; knit garments tend to stretch anyway—and, because seams add extra weight, they usually stretch most there. Avoid seam droop by folding knit garments flat rather than hanging them.

Shoes, particularly, need constant checking for heel and sole repairs and polishing. Check stockings for runs, and never wear stockings with reinforced heels and toes in open shoes.

Check underwear for proper fit and watch that it doesn't show underneath your clothing. Pay particular attention to handbags, briefcases, and their accessories (such as wallets, eyeglass cases, etc.) for signs of wear. All receive frequent handling, not to mention abuse. Don't hesitate to send them out for repair, redyeing, restitching, or whatever you can do to prolong their life and good looks.

Since gloves soil so easily, keep your eye on them. And, if you wear foundation makeup, check all collars regularly for makeup.

Certain fabrics tend to develop problems, too. Watch velour, velvet, and corduroy for a matted or "sat-out" look. When dry cleaning no longer rectifies this, donate the problem articles to charity. As gabardine gets elderly, it can develop quite a shine (some cleaners have a special process for dealing with this; ask about it). Meltons and other heavy, furry wools tend to wear first at their folds—sleeve ends and hems particularly. Wool or synthetic sweaters can pill—attack gently with a clothes brush. And dark colors will probably need a regular going-over with a lint brush.

If you perspire heavily, you may want to experiment with different kinds of dress shields. Dark or deeply colored silks and knits are particularly prone to color damage from perspiration and/or deodorants.

A properly set up closet or other clothing storage area goes a long way toward cutting down on ironing time, but if you have a very small apartment or inadequate storage space—and so many of us do— you might as well reconcile yourself to keeping your iron or steamer handy if you want to look your best.

Even if the cleaner has pressed your clothing, a crowded closet may mean you should always leave time to touch things up yourself.

Like most things, grooming and clothing care are easier if you keep them up on a regular basis. And there is nothing to substitute for the results: a clean, confident, cared-for appearance.

CHAPTER TEN

Conservative Chic on a Shoestring

ven if you have a very limited amount of money to spend on your clothes, you can build a conservative chic look if you are willing to put time and thought into it. And, because conservatively chic clothing does not go out of style, it is the ideal choice for a limited clothing budget.

To get the ultimate out of your budget, and the most elegance out of the clothes you buy with it, you need to become something of a fanatic about coordination. Never buy anything that does not go with everything, or almost everything, you have or are planning to get in cut, color, or pattern. Be extremely picky—you want only the simplest and most versatile shapes in the most becoming and flexible colors. Keep pattern to an absolute minimum and work with solids as much as possible to make coordination easier.

On a limited budget, everything you buy is that much more important. Stick to personal classics and a few really flattering colors. Avoid such strongly specific looks as will make you (and others) conscious of the fact that you "wore that last time."

To save yourself both time and money, really think through each purchase: Where and when will you be able to wear it? What else will it go with? Can you add or subtract layers for differing temperatures? Will it require its own special accessories? Don't buy it if it does. Will it work with your coat; or, if it *is* your coat, will it work over everything? Is it of a quality that will both look good and last? Will it be too expensive to clean or care for?

Shopping for a conservatively chic look on a tight budget is the opposite of impulse shopping. Before you ever set foot in a store, you need to have defined what it is you are looking for and why. That way, you can spend your time looking for exactly what you need at a price you can afford (the last part can be time-consuming), rather than wandering aimlessly looking for something to strike you.

Although limited funds may make sales and discount stores look very appealing, you need a strong character to come out of these with what you went in for. Don't be seduced by "bargains." It is better to buy one piece of clothing that looks just right on you and works with everything you have, at regular price—even if that price seems high—than to be seduced by sales and discounts into buying three less-than-perfect items for the same amount. When you shop in sales and discount stores, it's a good idea to keep reminding yourself what you came in for if you don't want to throw your money away.

The other problem about sale merchandise is that it's marked down near the end of a season when there is less of a selection. Of course, if you are lucky, you may find exactly the sweater that will go with all your pants and skirts, but if you are looking for a sweater to go with so many different pieces, you will have a better chance of finding it at the beginning of the season when there is more to choose from. And again, you are better off with that one sweater that works with five different pieces than with two for the same amount that work with one piece each.

Unless you have real confidence in a salesperson, never let his or her opinion sway your own good judgment. You know what you already have in your wardrobe and what your life is like; the salesperson probably does not. Develop confidence in your own selectivity and taste. And the same goes for shopping with a friend. *You* will be wearing the clothes you buy, so you must feel happy with them.

If your clothing budget is severely limited, and what you already have looks like an accumulation of odds and ends, try to find the one piece that could pull it all together into the semblance of a wardrobe.

If you are a woman with young children who is just entering or re-entering the job market, or if you have spent the last few years as a student and suddenly need more serious clothes, what should you buy first if you can only afford one purchase? It's probably a jacket. Buy the nicest-looking jacket you can afford to give odd skirts, pants, blouses, T-shirts, and sweaters a more dressed look. And remember: A jacket is not synonymous with a blazer. Even if blazers look good on you, they might not be the best choice in this instance: first, because a well-constructed blazer is expensive and you may not be able to afford a good one; and, second, because the shape of a blazer may not be versatile enough to work with all your odds and ends. It may be too formal-looking for what you are starting out with, unless it is unconstructed. There are other jackets that may offer more versatility for the money you have to spend: a cardigan jacket with kimono sleeves and no closing, a sweater-jacket, or maybe even an overshirt that pulls over the head. What you want is the finished look that the right top layer can give to a wide assortment of underlayers.

If you are struggling for a suited-up look on a budget that does not allow you to purchase three beautifully tailored suits, it may help to keep in mind that a suit doesn't really have to be one to look like one. In my book, a suit is any three pieces, two of which match. That means jacket and skirt could match with a contrasting blouse (the traditional suit), or blouse and skirt could match with a contrasting jacket, or blouse and jacket could match with a contrasting skirt. If your pieces are all conservatively cut, you'll be surprised how dignified and suitlike the last two combinations will look. You may even come to prefer them to the traditional suit!

If you already have a wonderfully versatile jacket, you might turn your attention to a bone-simple and beautifully cut skirt or pair of pants to give your clothes the look of a wardrobe. Try a straight dirndl in your neutral, and put it together with your odds and ends of tops and your versatile jacket or other top layer. Or, buy a well-cut pair of trousers in your neutral, if trousers look good on you and you can wear them to work or whatever you are branching out into.

If a style works for you, don't hesitate to buy it in other colors that flatter you, too. Such standardization is only boring if you make it so. If you tend to wear the same shapes in clothing, and you vary the look with your accessories, you will have a signature look rather than a uniform. A signature look is a very nice thing to have, because it's a kind of fashion personality.

If money is a problem, but you lust after the beauty of designer creations, don't despair—learn to re-create this look inexpensively by studying what makes it so special.

I do this many times a season for my personal clients when they either can't afford the designer creation, or it wouldn't work for them. I remember one woman in particular, a psychotherapist, who only looked her best in vibrant medium tones. While researching her wardrobe, I had seen in a store the most beautiful Geoffrey Beene suit that probably cost five times what she could afford to spend. It was a simply and gracefully cut jacket and skirt in a lightweight red wool gabardine. The blouse was a medium purple dull silk with moss green trim on the collar and a bunch of violets at the throat. While not the most versatile outfit, it was one of the most beautiful suits I have ever seen, and it would have looked incredibly beautiful on my client, but it was extremely expensive.

So I went about re-creating what I could excerpt from the Geoffrey Beene suit for my client's wardrobe. As color was the major point here, I put together a very simply cut red suit, a very simply cut blue-violet suit, a white linen blouse-jacket, a blue-violet summer pullover, one royal blue and one cherry silk short-sleeve shirt, and a bunch of violets that could be worn with everything. It wasn't Geoffrey Beene, but my client ended up with a designer look.

When you see a designer garment or outfit you love, try to analyze what is special about it. Is it the color? If it is, see if you can find those colors for yourself in other, less expensive pieces. If you pick pieces that are cut in a way that flatters you and you re-create what was beautiful about the designer outfit—the color—you may end up with an ensemble that is actually more becoming to you than the designer original would have been.

Check to see if the intricacy or the simplicity of the cut is what appeals to you. Intricate cuts are hard to re-create inexpensively, but simple cuts may not be. If you are willing to spend the time looking, you may be able to get the same feeling with simple shapes that complement your own.

Or, it could be pattern or texture—look carefully at how the designer combines them. You probably won't be able to duplicate what the designer has done, but you can translate it and adapt it to your own purposes.

In the end, if you master the information in this book, you become your own designer. Every season you select, translate, and adapt what is finest, most beautiful, most enduring to your own looks and needs. That is *Conservative Chic.*